# WHEN GOOD ENOUGH IS PERFECT

*A Veterinarian's Guide to Change,*
*Acceptance, and Letting Go*

**Cynde Gardner, DVM**

Cynde Gardner, DVM
# WHEN GOOD ENOUGH IS PERFECT

**A Veterinarian's Guide to Change, Acceptance, and Letting Go**

By Cynde Gardner

**ISBN:** 978-1-7364095-0-3

First Printing: January 2021

Cynde Gardner, DVM

Cynde@BrightPaths.com

(800) 278-0659

www.BrightPaths.com

Dr. Cynde Gardner is available to speak at your veterinary practice, association meeting, or other conference event on a variety of topics related to caring for the people who care for animals. Call (800) 278-0659 for booking information.

# Dedication

To all you perfectionists out there who deeply believe that something not done perfectly makes you a "failure", I can tell you there is a wonderful world on the other side waiting for you when you discover that sometimes good enough is perfect. I am living and thriving in that world now. In fact, proof of this is that I've published this perfectly imperfect book for the whole world to read. It's such a relief to know I don't have to be perfect every minute of every day. My wish is that you become willing to dip your toe into this new and welcoming world, testing the waters yourself. You may well be surprised at what you find!

To my husband, Eric – for your infinite patience and support. You needled, cajoled and down-right pushed me to actually write this. You always believe in me. Thank you.

# About the Author

Hi, I'm Cynde,

I am on a mission to transform the lives of veterinarians and other professionals. To nurture positive change. As a retired veterinarian, it breaks my heart to see the crisis of excessive stress, depression and suicide that plagues veterinarians and their staff.

A serious car accident resulted in a chronic pain syndrome where I lost much of the use of my right arm and hand. This effectively ended my career as a practicing veterinarian. After years of depression, pain, and wanting to end it all, I discovered the power of the mind-body connection.

I founded Bright Paths, a hypnotherapy, stress reduction and integrative success coaching practice to support others dealing with challenging life situations. Combining the skills and experience from my veterinary years with my years as a board-certified hypnotist and integrative success coach, I have developed simple, powerful and sustainable lifetime tools that can be used to reduce stress and create positive change, helping professionals reignite their passion for life.

Are you ready to move your life <u>From Frazzled to Dazzled</u>?
Reach out to me, I am a resource for you.

**CYNDE GARDNER, DVM, BCH**
**INTEGRATIVE SUCCESS COACH**

www.brightpaths.com

(800) 278-0659

Willingness, acceptance, and forgiveness are some of the most powerful words in the world. When their meaning is understood and applied with regularity, there will be wonderful changes in your life. – Dr. Cynde Gardner

# Acknowledgements

This book would not have been possible without the following people. My deep gratitude to you cannot be fully expressed.

Marie Maccagno – for your gentle, yet firm, guidance throughout the writing process, helping me to tap into the old darkness and bring the true blessings into the words on these pages.

Dr. Frank Whiting – for giving me five minutes of crying time and insisting on five minutes of laughing time that day you only had ten minutes before a meeting.

Doc Watts – for being such a kind and gentle leader.

Dr. Marty Fineman – for firing me - yes, I am truly grateful. You taught me so much.

Dr. Joe P. Morgan – for the support, guidance and friendship during my graduate school years.

Dr. Perry Cupps – for believing in me when others didn't. I'm glad I was able to make you proud!

Dr. Foster Lasdon – for your unwavering patience and for laughing so hard with me the day I figured it out.

Linda Doerksen – for being the best office manager, head technician and friend anyone could ask for. Through you, we thrived.

There are many others who provided inspiration, patience, insight and more that resulted in this iteration of me. My love, respect and appreciation for you has no bounds. I wish I could list you all, but that list would surely be longer than the book itself.

# A Note from Dr. Peter Weinstein

This book was written about me....that was the first thought that I had as I perused the pages. Although the details are different, my life from wannabe veterinarian to veterinary student to veterinarian to hospital owner to burnout and wanting to leave the profession has so many parallels to what Dr Gardner describes. If the story emulates mine it will emulate yours.

As I was going through many of the same issues identified, we didn't have names for them and we had even less resources to help us out. Cynde identifies them; gives the names; explains their roots and provides tools to use to address them and work to deal with them or best yet eliminate them.

Self-awareness is a short fall of many healthcare providers and their teams as they focus on taking care of others to their own detriment. Sometimes it takes a trauma or chronic pain or a feeling of wanting to give it all up to get someone to take action. There have been very few resources in the veterinary field written by veterinarians for veterinary teams. Very few tools that you can tap into that provide self-help opportunities.

Cynde has pulled away the curtain and encouraged us to look at all of our warts, scars, and ugliness by sharing her personal warts, scars and ugliness. Her pain is our pain. And instead of being self-critical, the easy thing to do, she has helped us to be self-aware by using easily relatable stories. And she has let us know that it is OK not to be perfect; that the Imposter Syndrome is omnipresent; and that perfection is the enemy to success.

Reality sucks. But when you have a means with which to deal with it, it can suck less. Share in Cynde's story. Feel her (your) pain. And relate to the way that she re-imagined herself and how you can reimagine yourself, too. When you get done with this quick read, the next time you look in the mirror you will see the beauty that is YOU.

Peter Weinstein, DVM, MBA
Executive Director, SCVMA
Colleague, co-worker, friend for decades

# Table of Contents

# Foreword

When *Good Enough is Perfect* is a perfect book! This book provides the internal resources so many of us need to not only get the ball rolling, but keep it rolling. When Dr. Gardner sent me the manuscript for this book, I was not planning to read it in one fell swoop, but I did. Cynde writes not only from her experience as a veterinarian, but also as a hypnotherapist, and her insights are applicable to any helping profession, and even to people who simply want to move forward in life regardless of their vocation.

This book is good! Dr. Gardner shares raw insight from her own life experiences, and anyone struggling to find serenity can find it in the pages of this book. She writes about her chronic pain, both physical and emotional, and her discovery of real-world solutions can be a lesson for all of us.

With concise language and clear explanations this book provides a key to all successful change. Successful change creates lasting change. In my own book, I shared strategies for business leaders to create sustaining change, seeing this as a hallmark of leadership success. Dr. Gardner believes something similar: within our own lives lasting change is the hallmark of success. Being able to change, despite circumstances remaining similar, is a key to lasting success.

I found that this book was supported by both research and statistics, and the special attention to the power of words and thoughts is explained in the context of how to use our inner dialog and thoughts as a starting point for putting all the pieces together again.

Every page of this book seems to yield doable strategies for getting it done and doing it good enough so that things are perfect. In short, this book is an actions strategy guidebook you can use in your work, your home, and in the real world. Thank you, Dr. Gardner, for providing such a helpful book that addresses how despite a difficult world, we can make our experience perfect!

Dr. Richard K. Nongard, LMFT Author of *Viral Leadership: Size the Power of Now to Create Lasting Change*

Katy, Texas 2021

# Introduction

This book was written from my perspective as a veterinarian. My original intention was to support veterinarians, technicians, and others in the animal-care field – to bring them hope and provide proven tools to help them on their path to personal and professional satisfaction. As more and more people heard about and read my manuscript, I received input that it would be excellent for medical doctors, nurses, therapists, and potentially anyone working in a caregiving position. Some of the specifics might be different, but it is fairly easy to substitute a comparable situation into the places where veterinary-specific examples are used.

I also hope that this book will offer some insight to those not in the medical fields about the behind-the-scenes challenges faced by those who dedicate their lives to caring for others – the challenges hidden under that professional façade.

And for those who still doubt it, yes, veterinarians are full doctors. They have gone through the rigorous schooling, testing of both their book knowledge and practical skills, licensing, and continuing education requirements of anyone awarded the right to practice medicine. They simply learn it all for multiple species of animals rather than just one.

Veterinarians and medical doctors, as well as their staff, are merely mortal humans with follies and foibles and lives of their own. With wishes and hopes and dreams they want to bring into reality. People who have dedicated, by choice, their working lives to the care of others, be they human or animal. People who are perfectly imperfect and doing the best they possibly can with what is available to them at any given time.

To whomever chooses to read this, I hope that it stimulates thoughtful conversations. That it fosters understanding and compassion for those in medicine. Ideally, this book will provide a catalyst for positive change in the animal and human medical fields — change that must start within each individual.

I hope to not only shed light on the crucial need to create working environments that are nourishing and fulfilling, but also to bring awareness that there are proven tools for change available to you and to those you love from someone who understands the field. I want to share that there is hope, even in the darkest of hours. And I will show you how you can learn more and get the help you need to move successfully beyond the darkness.

You matter. Your wishes, hopes, and dreams are important. You have the right to a full, happy life. You, too, can move from frazzled to dazzled by your life.

Although the pronoun "he" is used in this book, it is used generically. Please substitute the pronoun of your choice as you enjoy this adventure.

# Chapter 1

## A BRIEF SUMMARY OF THE HERO'S JOURNEY

I was introduced to the concept of the hero's journey a few years ago at a retreat. It was originally described in 1949 by Joseph Campbell. The hero's journey is not only a story structure for writing; it is a universal story arc that appears in diverse cultures around the world. It classically refers to a story in which the main character (hero) starts within their ordinary, familiar world. They are living life as they know it, with limited awareness that a problem may soon arise.

Then something changes, as life does, creating discomfort, dis-ease, or dissatisfaction. The change may come from the external world or from deep within the hero. It seems he is being pulled in multiple directions. He develops an increased awareness that something isn't right. Things are not working the way they used to. Something needs to change. The hero now has a dilemma.

Being human, it is common for the hero to ignore the dilemma that has arisen. He pretends it doesn't exist. He resists the internal or external push to change. He may fear the unknown – the uncertainty – and perceive potential danger, so he tries to hang onto his old, normal, familiar world. But the change is happening anyway. It is real. And as the hero continues to fight the change, his personal discomfort increases. His stress escalates. He feels his safety challenged as time and events alter what he has always considered normal.

Eventually, he must begin to accept the fact that change is happening, whether he likes it or not. He can either fight it and be miserable or learn to adapt in ways that will allow him to not just survive but also thrive.

In the hero's journey, the hero then comes across a more worldly person who has the ability to guide, teach, advise, or provide tools to the hero as he journeys through the unknown and uncertainty of change. When the hero agrees to learn from this mentor or coach, he develops the skills to navigate not only this change, but also future change with courage and wisdom.

In accepting this relationship, the hero commits to moving forward in life in a strong, positive way. He accepts that he must let go of the past and venture into new, unfamiliar territory with its unknown rules.

It will not always be smooth going in this new world. The hero will be tested and challenged many times. He must sort out who his true allies and enemies are as he learns the rules in this new world. He experiments with new conditions in his changing world.

The hero may never feel ready to face the tests and ordeals the new world brings about. The big changes he faces may be life-threatening or just appear life-threatening. The hero confronts death, or his worst fears, and emerges with a new perspective – a new life. With this comes the acceptance of the consequences and benefits of the new life.

The hero now receives the reward for his hard work. He possesses the riches won by facing his worst fears or even death. These riches are strength, wisdom, courage, self-confidence, and faith to thrive in life. Because it is newfound, the reward is still at risk, though. It remains at risk until it is firmly cemented into the belief system of the hero.

There will be new challenges to the riches or rewards he has attained. The strength, wisdom, courage, self-confidence, and faith he has gained may be harshly tested as he navigates this road. The hero digs deeply into himself to survive the tests and emerges with these riches bound tightly into his beliefs.

He develops mastery in this new, changed world, and the new world now becomes his regular, ordinary world where he thrives. Through his actions, the struggles and resistance he experienced at the beginning of the journey are resolved.

As I began to apply the hero's journey format to my own writing, I realized that the true hero's journey is the one each of us lives daily. The pattern or format used to create engaging stories for people to read, watch, or tell simply reflects everyday life in an easy-to-understand way.

The story may be a snapshot of one specific period of time or the complete story of someone's life. It is told in an engaging way to capture the reader's attention. One reader may have one reaction to the story, while another reader may have a completely different response. This is desirable and due to the uniqueness of each of us and our unique perceptions of life.

How true this also is for everyday real life. We perceive it in our own way, while others may perceive something completely differently. The hero's journey format not only provides a step-by-step structure for writing a story; it provides a step-by-step structure for accepting change in our lives and thriving as the world evolves.

## The Hero's Journey

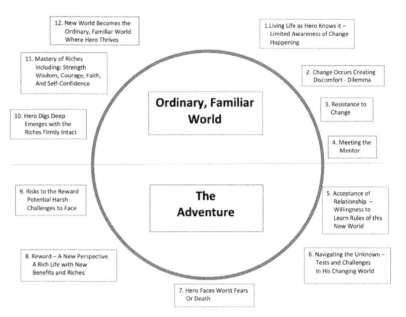

I will share with you as much as I can within the confines of this book about *how* I grew and changed from a negative, disbelieving, unhappy person into one who truly loves life. I will share some specific tools that I used successfully to make this transition a reality. Then I will give you information on how **you** can take action **now** to move toward creating the life you desire. Use this book as a starting point and to give you reassurance that if this crazy lady can change, you can, too.

In the book, I begin with my "ordinary world" as a veterinary doctor, using my personal experiences and those of some of my clients to illustrate key points. Please note that where I use examples from those I've worked with, their anonymity is completely maintained.

You are invited to reflect on what I describe. See what you identify with and open your mind to new and immensely successful ways to take your life back – to begin making positive changes in your life *immediately*.

If you are feeling trapped in a cycle of endless work, frustration, not feeling understood, and no rest, this book is for you!

If you've "tried everything" with no real change or success, grab this book, a cup of tea, find a comfy chair, and dig in. It will help guide you on your own road to a happier life.

**The Secret to Change is to Focus All Your Energy, Not into Fighting the Old, But on Building the New. - Socrates**

# Chapter 2

## Where Veterinary Medicine Stands Today

Veterinarians deal with a lot of unusual things that people in other fields of work don't encounter. It's not all playing with adorable puppies and kittens when they come in for their first health exam and vaccinations. Sadly, the high rate of depression, addiction, and suicide among veterinarians and others in the various medical fields continues to rise. Many veterinarians and their staff are contemplating or have already left the field because of the unrelenting stress. Too many have chosen to leave life altogether.

We still see this increase in addiction, depression, and suicide continuing, despite all of the research and information now available. Most of the information currently available is about the facts of the situation, the history, rather than solutions and prevention processes. I hope to change this emphasis, beginning now. While some of this book presents the facts, using my history and the history of those I've worked with as examples, the emphasis is on how to recognize and change your perception of the facts of your life, allowing you to create the life you desire. In other words, this book is solution oriented.

# Chapter 3

## My Personal Story

I wish I had been less idealistic and understood more about the medical field before I became a practicing veterinarian. It may or may not have changed my mind about choosing this career path, but I certainly would have been better prepared for the reality and better able to handle it.

I started my animal love affair when I was five years old. I was to undergo surgery to remove my tonsils. I was a little scared, mostly because I didn't understand what was going on. However, my fear quickly turned to pleasure when the nurse gave me ice cream when I woke up. Then, it got even better. Because I was "so good" for the whole procedure, my parents got me my first puppy. Chica and I grew up together, and I loved her madly. This was my first memorable introduction to the concept of how important it was in life to "be good." In my child's mind, I thought the better I was, the more wonderful my life would be. If I was "perfect," then life would be perfect.

It didn't take me long to become fascinated by the concept of raising and taking care of animals. I had various critters as pets growing up – mice, rabbits, guinea pigs, chinchillas, birds, a few lizards, a snake and so on. In high school, I immediately joined the Future Farmers of America (FFA). I raised Suffolk sheep, even bringing my ewe to our suburban home, much to my parent's chagrin. Then, I got my first horse. I was the quintessential horse-crazy teenager who never outgrew that phase.

I chose an Animal Science major for my undergraduate degree, and yes, my horse did go to college with me. It was there that I began to get serious about making animals my career. At that point, I was sure I would be a large animal veterinarian. After all, I was horse-crazy!

I received my bachelor's and master's degrees in Animal Science with an emphasis on reproductive physiology, then I went on to Veterinary School. In vet school, I gravitated more toward small animals, which surprised me. I discovered that I really wanted my horses to be where I got my break and me-time, rather than working with them professionally all day and then coming home to feel they were also "chores" I had to deal with at night.

Then, one day, I graduated. I was a doctor. Funny, I didn't feel any different than I had the day before, when I was still just a student. Now, there were those terrifying licensing board exams to pass. I did, and suddenly, I was a licensed veterinarian. While it was exciting, it was difficult to wrap my mind around the concept that I was a licensed doctor. All the paperwork and legal documents said I was ready to practice medicine. I was now the one responsible for the health and well-being of the precious pets that people entrusted to me. Was I good enough for this? After all, I was still just me; the same me that I was the day before I graduated or became licensed.

One of our neighbors owned a veterinary hospital near my parents' home, so I started my first job there. I loved it. I learned so much. I asked questions constantly. I was so excited to learn everything I could as quickly as I could. Apparently, I was so new and excited about this work that I didn't read the situation in the hospital well. While I was young, enthusiastic, and quite the eager beaver, the senior partner in the group was at the stage where he wanted to wind down his practice career. What he really wanted was someone who, once they learned the running of his particular practice, could step in and take over for him. A bouncy, enthusiastic sponge for information simply wasn't his cup of tea.

I drove him crazy with my enthusiasm and constant stream of questions. Eventually, he became so frustrated with me that even his wife said it was time to let me go. I was completely clueless when the two doctors brought me in, sat me down, and told me I was fired. I was shocked! I was embarrassed. I lost confidence in my skills. I thought I wasn't good enough. I doubted everything about myself. Me as a person, my knowledge, my skills, everything I had worked so hard to build crumbled down around me. Would I ever be able to find another job after being fired from my first one? Who would want me?

Another veterinary friend was looking to hire someone, so I immediately joined him. He was fine with my questions, but I learned to tone things down a bit. I was still just as anxious to learn and become the best, but my approach was much different this time.

After a few months working at the new practice, I realized that I had accepted the position out of desperation. I hadn't taken time to learn enough about the practice's philosophy before jumping in. I began waking up to the fact that it wasn't a good fit for me. But what was I supposed to do now? I had been fired from my first job for over-enthusiasm, and now I knew I had jumped into a situation that really wasn't good for me. I summoned my courage to give notice and found a completely different style of practice that would support me as a newly-minted, gung-ho veterinarian.

I am grateful I was able to remain friends with each of the doctors I worked with, and we have fun reminiscing, joking, and laughing when we meet at conferences. I do feel blessed for the time and education they offered me.

During this time, I also underwent an experience I wouldn't wish on anyone. My boyfriend at the time, Glenn, was involved in a serious car accident. The accident occurred while he was overseas, so I couldn't get to him immediately. Over the next week, as I made arrangements to travel, I kept getting regular calls telling me how one organ or another had failed, but they kept "getting him back for me." His EEG suggested severe brain damage, later called catastrophic, irreversible brain damage, but they were trying their best to "save him for me." As I frantically tried to get to him, he continued to fail, bounce back, fail, bounce back, fail, bounce back. My medical knowledge felt like a burden, since I understood only too well what was happening and I could do nothing about it. I was on an emotional roller coaster. After over a week in the hospital, he passed away.

I felt helpless. Hopeless. Lost.

The combination of Glenn's tragic death shortly after I had been fired from my first job and had decided to leave my second one really did a number on me emotionally. I was a mess. I looked for any distraction to keep from thinking about my life. Anything to avoid dealing with the grief I had experienced during those months. It wasn't until years later that I was diagnosed with PTSD. Of course, I would have denied it at the time, anyway.

My next career move was joining a multi-doctor, multi-hospital group. I really enjoyed practice; in fact, I thrived in it. It was a busy group, so I could throw myself into the work and not have time to think about anything else. Since I was single and new to the area, I had all the time in the world to devote to my passion. Yes, the hours were long, we were sometimes short-handed, and some of the clients were a bit challenging. But I was young, a go-getter, and completely devoted to my career. I threw myself into work, not thinking about my personal life or health. I made myself available and accepted as much overtime as they could throw at me. It was a great way to hide from reality, even though I didn't realize at the time that I was hiding. Another thing I would have denied at the time.

I believed I could do it all. I believed I had to do it all, and being the new kid on the block, I wanted to show the bosses that I could handle everything they gave me. Since I had not had great experiences with my first two jobs, I desperately wanted to prove my worth to the group and be perceived as a competent doctor. It was clearly the "new kid on the block" or new graduate syndrome. I was like a puppy panting and bouncing around their feet, looking for the smallest sign of approval.

I stretched my limits often and saw it as a learning experience and an opportunity to grow. After all, the more time I spent working, the more experience I got so I could be a "good" doctor. Remember, my experience with receiving the gift of Chica when I was five had shown me the importance of "being good." I really wanted to be good! In fact, my goal was to be one of the best. My life outside of work was pretty much non-existent, but I didn't think that mattered. I was working in a career I loved, doing what I was trained to do. What more could I ask for at this stage of my life?

Then I caught a cold. It turned into bronchitis. I knew I needed a couple of days off to recover, but we were short-handed. So when the administrators were reluctant to give me time off, my guilt about leaving them even shorter handed made me all too eager to push through and keep working. How could I let them down? They needed me. I was an important part of their practice. What a heady feeling! I was doing good work, helping people and pets, and making a difference. Of course, I continued to work. Until, that is, I literally collapsed at the office. I couldn't breathe.

The emergency room diagnosis was pneumonia. Bilateral and extensive. I was told to go home and rest. When I continued to worsen rather than improve at home, my regular doctor suggested I should consider being admitted to the hospital. He settled for me staying with my parents while I recovered, since he knew my mother well and was confident that she would watch me like a hawk. She certainly did!

After I had been off work for a little over a week, my employer called to advise me that if I wasn't back at work the following Monday, they would have to replace me. That meant less than two weeks of recovery time from pneumonia. At that point, I was still sleeping in a recliner that kept me somewhat upright because I couldn't breathe while lying flat.

Once again, my guilt and my sense of responsibility pulled me back to work. I had made a commitment that I was determined to honor. I had difficulty breathing, and my cough was still nasty. Even though I had to take regular breaks, sitting down to catch my breath, I had made a commitment. How could I appear weak, perhaps a failure? I was convinced that my reputation was on the line. I was driven by my need to prove myself.

Miraculously, I didn't relapse. However, I had a long and difficult recovery. You see, in addition to our regular day-time hours, every doctor took after-hours calls on a rotating schedule. The on-call doctor took calls for all three hospitals and was expected to go to whichever hospital received the call. That often meant traveling many miles between each of the hospitals in a single night to address all of the emergency calls. We would then report to our assigned hospital the next morning for our regular daytime hours. I was exhausted. But I had been taught that self-care was selfish, self-indulgent. So I just kept going.

After a couple years of working in this challenging but wonderfully educational environment, a friend persuaded me that it was time to buy my own hospital. This idea appealed to me, so I bought a practice that had been failing miserably for the previous few years. I began the long, upward battle to turn the hospital around. With a lot of work, long hours, being on call every night, and the help of an amazing office manager, we built a hospital I was proud of. It was exhausting but so rewarding.

As the practice grew, I also began teaching classes at a local college for veterinary technicians. My hospital provided a practical experience location for students and the occasional newly graduated veterinarian. One day, a newly graduated veterinarian I had been working with was driving me crazy. Didn't they teach them anything in vet school anymore? My patience grew thin.

Then, suddenly, I remembered how I had driven my first boss crazy as a new graduate. That evening, I called one of the two doctors from my first job and asked him if I had really been that bad when I first graduated. I told him what I was experiencing with the new graduate, and apologized profusely for what I had put him and the senior partner through.

After he stopped his deep belly-laughing (which took quite a while), we had the most wonderful talk. He reminded me that I was, in fact, a good, qualified doctor, even then. I was just inexperienced. Veterinarians don't graduate with the all-important experience we will have after ten, twenty, or thirty years of practice. We will never have all of the experience to know everything about everything. Each doctor has their own experience based on the cases that walk in the door. It's the "practice" of medicine, not the "perfection" of medicine. This conversation gave me a new perspective on things, which benefited both me and the new graduates I worked with.

While I will remember him and the pep talk forever, I wasn't completely ready to accept that belief for myself. My willingness to accept and forgive myself hadn't kicked in quite yet. Self-doubt and self-criticism were still my foundations.

I kept up this pace for several more years, building up a strong client base, continuing to improve my knowledge, and studying to learn new skills to bring into my practice. I was doing what I had set out to do in life. But slowly, over time, my enthusiasm began to decline and my fatigue level increased. Looking back, my older, wiser self would have hired another veterinarian at that point. However, I still had the mentality that I should be able to handle it all. It was my practice, and I was proud of it. In my mind, the only way I could be sure my clients and patients received the quality of care I wanted for them was if I saw to it myself. Then, and only then, would I know that things were done "right."

Eventually, things that would have previously rolled off me began to frustrate and irritate me. The unrelenting, daily stress of dealing with life-and-death situations with the animals I cared for, dodging being bitten and scratched (and often that was just by the owners), avoiding being pooped and peed on, and trying to avoid being hit when emptying those pesky anal glands drained my energy.

Euthanasia was especially problematic for me. Whether it's for financial or medical reasons, it's still the intentional taking of a life. I agreed to first do no harm when I entered the field. I became very attached to many of the pets I treated. They sometimes felt like my beloved pets that I let someone else take home and care for. Regardless of the reason for the euthanasia, it could be heartbreaking.

Dealing with all of the state and federal regulations that impact a veterinary business, routine business management, taxes, landlords, continuing education, and inventory felt increasingly overwhelming. Added to that were the typical demands of hiring, firing, and supervising employees. Working with a staff of people who are also caregivers by nature meant they tended to be more sensitive and emotional – and sometimes challenging to work with. When the staff wasn't stepping up and doing their jobs "properly," I felt the need to step in and either do it myself or micromanage them. Otherwise, the work might not get done "right."

Daily encounters with emotional and demanding pet owners and the highly charged emotional combination of pets and money can take a toll. There is often a lack of respect and appreciation for what veterinarians do because of the pervasive lack of understanding by the general public of what goes into being a veterinarian. As mentioned above, many people don't believe that veterinarians are "real" doctors. Sadly, this perception is perpetuated even further with the amount of misinformation available on the internet.

Emotional blackmail by clients can be grueling. Clients sometimes said that if I really cared about animals, I wouldn't charge so much to take care of them. If I had any heart at all, I would do this for free. Why was I being so cold and cruel as to leave them with no choice but to euthanize their precious puppy because they couldn't afford, or chose not to get, preventative care for them? Now that it had parvo, or another preventable disease, they couldn't afford to treat it.

I lost track of the number of times I was told, "You're only in it for the money." Never mind the incredible overhead I had as a practice owner, the student loans I had to pay off, and oh yes, the fact that I needed to pay for a place to live and support myself. Never mind that I chose caring for animals as my career because of my deep love for them. A quality income is necessary and deserved for veterinarians and all medical professionals.

The joy I felt during my early years in practice slowly became a distant memory. I still loved working with the animals, but the other parts of practice were becoming drudgery. Self-doubt crept in and began trampling me with its ever-growing feet. Bigger and bigger feet, it seemed. Walking all over my self-confidence.

My sense of self-worth faded. I began to feel betrayed and desperate. Something had to change, but what? Here, I thought I was in my dream job. I had worked so hard to get into veterinary school, and then to learn everything I needed to graduate and pass the boards. After successfully getting into practice, I discovered there was much to veterinary medicine that I had never been trained for. Never understood. Never even dreamed of. The stress kept building. I felt trapped by my choices. Guilty for no longer being sure that I wanted to be a veterinarian. I was consumed by guilt, self-doubt, and stress.

I didn't understand that I simply lacked the proper emotional tools to deal with managing a business. I was well-trained in medicine and doing a good job there. However, the other aspects of the field were completely foreign to me. It was a classic case of I didn't know what I didn't know. I knew I needed to do continuing education to keep my technical skills sharp and stay up with the new advances in medicine, but I didn't understand the need for continuing education for soft skills such as self-care, emotional intelligence, and client and staff interactions. The medicine came easily for me, but those soft skills that allowed other veterinarians to thrive in the field were more elusive.

One particular day, I had an unexpected break during my lunch hour – something to be treasured, for sure! That meant I could run out quickly on an errand for my mother that I had planned to do after work, if I got off before the store closed. I headed out and never made it back for my afternoon clients. I was broadsided by an individual who ran a stop sign. My neck, arm, and hand were severely injured. As a result, I lost considerable use of my right arm and hand. After surgery on my hand and extensive physical therapy, my orthopedic surgeon said I was going to be one of those people who just falls through the cracks. He had handed me what felt like a life sentence when he advised me to get used to living with chronic pain and disability. Because of my injuries, I developed an unexplained chronic pain syndrome that was only identified years later as thoracic outlet syndrome (TOS).

The chronic pain syndrome was unrelenting, and much of my time during the following years was spent wearing my right shoulder as an earring due to the severity of the pain and muscle spasms. I tried to keep my hospital running but ultimately ended up selling it out of desperation. It was just too physically and emotionally painful to do the work any longer. Then, I tried several other ways to continue to practice that would hopefully be easier on my injured neck and arm. After all, what else was I trained to do? What could a youngish veterinarian do if not practice? Was I supposed to just walk away from it all?

I felt guilty about the help others had given to get me where I was. Guilty for having amassed student loan debt. Guilt made me keep trying to practice, knowing that if I left this career, I would be judged a failure. A quitter. Not good enough.

Eventually, I realized that I was being forced to retire due to my physical limitations and inability to practice any longer. That "life sentence" the orthopedic surgeon had given me was becoming a reality I couldn't continue to deny. It was so very hard to accept. Fear, anxiety, guilt, and depression ran rampant in me.

I struggled for several years, trying to find something I could do. I looked both inside the veterinary field and outside. There were a couple of government veterinary positions that were available, but that would require moving. Since I had just bought my dream home in my dream location a month before the accident, that wasn't an option.

On paper, I was overqualified for many things so I wouldn't even be considered, regardless of my willingness. Several potential employers said I would get bored and leave, or they couldn't pay me enough because of my degrees. The qualifications that I used to be so proud of felt not just useless, but a liability. I believed that my training was so focused and specialized that there was nothing else I was qualified to do. I felt trapped by my education, guilt, a sense of failure and of being a disappointment to family, friends, co-workers, clients, and myself – and just being a disappointment in general. Basically, I felt that my life no longer had any value.

My confidence was shot. I felt like I was taking up unnecessary space with nothing to contribute. I remember lying in bed one night watching the ceiling fan turn. As I watched it slowly rotate, I understood in that moment why some people consider suicide. Why they would feel that the world would be just fine, or maybe even better off, without them. They were a burden anyway. Useless. They can't do the one thing they were trained for – what they had planned and worked so hard to achieve. Watching the fan turn, I had all of these thoughts and more.

Suicide seemed a very logical choice to me. I gave ending my life serious thought that night. Watching the fan turn… Ways to do it. Watching the fan turn… Why do it. Watching the fan turn… When to do it. Watching the fan turn…

After some time, I had a pretty good plan in place. Then my thoughts traveled to my family. My parents. My pets. What would happen to them? I realized that suicide wasn't the best route for me. At least not right then. I could always circle back to it down the road if nothing else worked out. Perhaps after more appropriate planning.

# Chapter 4

# WILLINGNESS TO CHANGE – Embarking on the Journey

I started rethinking my future then. Suddenly, the pain of staying the same outweighed the pain and fear of change. I knew I disliked – heck, I *hated* – my life. I was miserable. I had no desire to continue living as things were. If I wasn't ready for suicide quite yet, what were my options? I sure hadn't found any good ones up to that point. All of the places I knew to look had netted nothing to improve my life. What was I supposed to do if everything I knew to try had failed?

I still had a small flicker of hope that there was something out there for me that I just couldn't see from my current perspective. I gingerly opened my mind to different avenues of work. Carefully testing the waters, I slowly explored a wider array of options for myself. Wow... was that a challenge!

I still believed that I had to do it all myself, or I would be considered a failure. I had to be the strong one. So this looking outside of my own toolbox for options was tough to swallow. How would others view me if I needed outside help? Eventually, even though I was afraid to be "found out," I did reach out for and accept help.

I was blessed shortly after that to begin working for VPI Pet Insurance. I discovered that there were other viable and productive uses for my knowledge beyond practice. Eventually, I even discovered that the knowledge I had accumulated wasn't just about veterinary medicine. It was about life. I had things to offer, both inside and outside of the medical field. I slowly began to understand through counselors, mentors, and coworkers that my options were wider than I ever could have dreamed on my own. I just had to be *willing* to see things from a different perspective.

Meanwhile, the chronic pain from thoracic outlet syndrome was exhausting. It's amazing how chronic pain impacts one's daily life. It is difficult for those not suffering from it to understand what a person with chronic pain experiences – the physical, mental, and emotional distress it causes. This invisible medical condition can wreak havoc on one's life.

I recall attending an event where I was in so much pain, it was physically impossible for me to sit in my chair and take notes. I paced the back of the room, trying to follow along and take notes with my head cranked down to the right and my shoulder pressed against my cheek because the pain and muscle spasms were so severe.

On one of the breaks, another attendee – a total stranger – approached me and offered to help. After confirming that what he suggested was legal, ethical, and moral, I agreed to give it a shot. I was miserable and willing to try almost anything. The thought of living this way for the rest of my life was daunting.

He was a hypnotist. He hypnotized me right there in the middle of the event, with everyone milling around. I was out of pain for the first time in fifteen years. I knew immediately that this was the start of something powerful, and I was about to embark on a new career. I wanted to share this solution with other chronic pain sufferers.

Now let me provide a little clarification here. Yes, I was out of pain – truly out of pain – for the first time in fifteen years. But did that mean the thoracic outlet syndrome magically disappeared? Did that mean all the built-up scar tissue had vanished? All of the hypertrophied muscles and atrophied muscles were suddenly normal, healthy, and functional? Of course not! I was out of pain; I was comfortable. I discovered for the first time in a long time that hope was realistic. I saw real ***hope*** for my future for the first time in over fifteen years. However, I realized that hope without action would get me nowhere.

Because of the effectiveness of the rudimentary hypnotic pain management tools I initially learned, I was able to move forward more comfortably and confidently. It began to look like that life sentence of chronic pain and disability might just get overturned. That hypnotist showed me how to use the power of my own mind to release the pain and stress. To break the fear–tension–pain cycle. To change my perspective. My mind and body responded well. Over time, I regained full function in my right arm and hand.

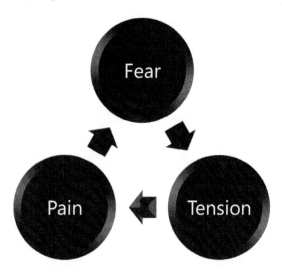

## THE KEY TO ALL SUCCESSFUL CHANGE

I discovered that I had the key to go from a life filled with debilitating stress, pain, anxiety, depression, and suicidal thinking to feeling optimistic and even happy. Yet, the circumstances of my life hadn't changed one bit. *Let me repeat that:* I discovered I had the key to go from a life filled with debilitating stress, pain, anxiety, depression, and suicidal thinking to feeling hopeful and even happy. ***Yet, the circumstances of my life hadn't changed one bit.***

I still, to this day, have TOS. I still face crazy-making, often unreasonable demands and challenges in my personal and professional life. The tools that I learned and now use regularly allowed me to create a happy, rewarding life – one that I am living and thriving in today.

***My perception had changed.*** **How I saw and lived my life circumstances changed.** My whole life changed when I became *open and willing* to change myself.

## SHARING THE GIFTS – The Reward

Given how much my life changed as a result of my willingness to open my mind to new possibilities, implementing hypnosis and other self-care modalities, and increasing my emotional intelligence, it became important for me to share with you what I've learned on my personal road back to physical, mental, emotional, and spiritual health. I continue to learn from my work with veterinarians, technicians, medical doctors, nurses, and other caregivers across the country. And I love that as I collaborate in helping and learning with others, I've developed new programs that help an even broader group of people.

When I was first introduced to hypnosis, I was skeptical. As a scientist, I believed that hypnotism was based on woo-woo. In my mind, the concept was, "Oh, just believe in this woo-woo stuff and it'll work for you." Dictionary.com defines woo-woo as "unconventional beliefs regarded as having little or no scientific basis, especially those relating to spirituality, mysticism, or alternative medicine."

I needed to understand the science behind the supposed woo-woo. I learned about the mind-body connection and the significant physiological impact of stress on the mind and body. I learned that the mind, including how we think and talk to ourselves, significantly impacts our physiology.

For example, you can change your heart rate and other bodily functions simply by thinking about it – by using the power of your own mind. Many still doubt this, but are you ready for a little proof?

Take a moment now and measure your heart rate. Got it? Good. Now think of a situation that *really* upsets you. Something that *really* makes you angry, gets your blood boiling, or frightens you terribly. Perhaps a child or pet in danger, thinking you might be downsized out of your job, or a cheating spouse. If you have trouble coming up with something quickly, just imagine you are in the dentist's chair and the doctor begins to drill on your painful tooth before the anesthetic has kicked in. Focus on it for a moment. The things you see. The sounds. The smells around you. Allow yourself to be wrapped up in that unpleasant, stressful thought. Now measure your heart rate again and see if it has changed. For most people, there will be a noticeable increase in the heart rate as a direct result of just thinking of something stressful. Notice that you were simply *thinking* about something stressful, not undergoing it or experiencing it in that moment. Your thoughts – not an actual event – triggered the increase in your heart rate,.

# CHAPTER 5.

# THOUGHTS HAVE POWER – The Placebo/Nocebo Effect

## The Power of Positive Thoughts

Science has been proving that the mind can heal the body for years. That supposed woo-woo stuff has a scientific name and has been well researched. Scientists call it the Placebo/Nocebo Effect. Research has documented the power of the brain, through your thoughts and beliefs, to make positive physiological and psychological changes in the body, including decreasing depression, stress, and anxiety.[1,2,3,4] In one study looking at the effects of hypnosis on immune system responses, hypnotized patients had significant alteration of the immune response.[5] This is highly significant, in that it documents that your thoughts have the power to create physiological changes. As Wayne Dyer suggests, when you change your thoughts, you change your life.[6]

The placebo effect is well documented to cause actual, positive physiological and psychological change. Healing. Yet, for the placebo effect to work, the only thing that changes is someone's thinking. Their expectations. Their beliefs. There is no actual treatment or therapy given. Individuals think themselves well. They believe it will happen, so it does.

In extensive studies, it has been shown that up to 80% of those given "sugar pills" (placebo) in trials recover without any active pharmacological treatment. Research also shows that the recovery time is typically shorter than that expected for the normal course of the injury or illness without treatment.

## Negative Thinking Also Has Power

Science has also documented the ability of the mind to create physical and mental illness. It is called the nocebo effect. In essence, you can think yourself sick. It is the ultimate in self-deception, creating a self-fulfilling prophecy.

My father was, sadly, a classic example of this. He had colon cancer. The doctors started him on chemotherapy, with the unfortunately required warnings about the *potential* side effects. He wasn't told about all of the potential side effects, due to the length of the list.

My father experienced *all* of the *potential* side effects he had been told about and *none* of the potential side effects he wasn't told about. He experienced the effects he was made aware of because he feared them and believed that – with a diagnosis of cancer and the stories of chemotherapy he had heard – he would experience these side effects and ultimately die anyway. His lack of awareness of the other side effects appeared to spare him from their effects.

He was also told that the average lifespan for someone with his diagnosis was six months. His memorial was six months to the day after he heard this. He never understood that "average" means that there are people on both sides of that number – many of whom live significantly longer with good quality lives, and some who recover completely. He heard "six months" and that's when he believed he would die. So he did.

Some may think that he was simply one of the cases that represented the lower end of the six-month average. Technically, that is true. However, living with him, watching and listening to his attitudes and his approach to the disease and treatment, I saw clearly that he believed he had six months to live and would suffer miserably during that time. He occasionally mentioned the amount of time he had left as the months went by, as if he was counting down. He created his reality based on the information he heard and believed to be literal and true.

This isn't to suggest that cancer isn't a fatal disease in many cases, or that cancer treatment is fun. I'm simply sharing an example of how the nocebo effect can negatively impact the quality of an individual's life just as effectively as the placebo effect can positively impact it. There are many documented cases of nocebo effects in the literature, especially when looking at control groups in studies for new drugs. In an article on WebMD, John Kelley, Ph.D., deputy director of Harvard Medical School's Program in Placebo Studies & Therapeutic Encounter says, "Whenever you look at any randomized control trials, it's surprising how similarly the side-effect profile for the placebo often mirrors the side-effect profile for the active [treatment]... It's the power of the imagination."[7] My, but the mind is powerful!

The nocebo effect is evident in cases of mental illness such as depression, chronic stress, and anxiety, too. People with a negative outlook on life tend to exhibit signs of depression and/or anxiety more frequently than those with a positive outlook.

As a result of my research, I also discovered that, even before the accident that precipitated my early, unplanned, yet often dreamed of retirement from veterinary practice, I suffered from imposter syndrome, compassion fatigue, and burnout. I allowed the nocebo effect of my own negative thinking to lure me into those beliefs. My mental health was a mess. The resultant chronic stress also took a toll on my body.

I was totally clueless about the power of the mind back then. Only with 20/20 hindsight was I able to understand what happened. I just thought I was weak – that I wasn't good enough. I didn't want others to think that I wasn't as knowledgeable or strong as they were. I didn't want to show how "weak" I thought I was.

Other veterinarians I knew seemed to handle everything just fine. They seemed so successful. I thought that I had to just power through, be strong, and do it all like everyone else *appeared* to be doing. I didn't understand back then that I had never learned how to manage the normal stress of practice – or even basic life.

I was running on empty but just kept putting one foot in front of the other. And Heaven forbid anyone should find out what was going on in my head – what I really thought about myself, about veterinary medicine, and about life in general. I was a total wreck inside while putting on a professional façade for the world. I wanted others to perceive me as being just as successful as they were, whether I believed it or not. It never occurred to me that others might experience similar feelings. I was sure it was just me. I didn't realize that I was judging the inside of myself by comparing myself to the outside presentation of others. I also didn't understand how dangerous, unfair, and damaging this self-judgment was.

Success is not always what you see on the outside.

I've learned over time that I am far from alone in my feelings. Many others silently struggle with the same or similar challenges as I did. Their outside façade, like mine, hides self-doubt, imposter syndrome, depression, anxiety, physical and emotional exhaustion, and much more.

If you're reading this book, I suspect you or someone you know may be currently suffering from the long-term nocebo effect of negative thinking. Learning and using the techniques I describe in this book may help you or a loved one prevent some of the damaging losses I've experienced along the way.

My desire to heal from chronic stress led me to do some research on what I was experiencing. Here are some interesting statistics on stress:

- WebMD states: "Stress symptoms vary greatly from one person to the next, but the most universal sign of stress is a feeling of being pressured or overwhelmed." Other symptoms include stomachaches, headaches, chest pains, nausea, and diarrhea, and a sensation of numbness or tingling in your hands, arms, and face, short temper, unexplained anger, dysfunctional sleep patterns and communication difficulty. [8]

- According to the Harvard Medical School, stress creates cognitive problems and a higher risk for Alzheimer's disease and dementia. "It's not uncommon to feel disorganized and forgetful when you're under a lot of stress. But over the long term, stress may actually change your brain in ways that affect your memory." [9]

- Dr. Oz states that up to 90% of doctor visits in the US are for stress-related illness. [10]

- Exposure to stress can disrupt function of the pre-frontal cortex, significantly impairing working memory. This elicits scattered thought, difficulty with focus and judgment errors that can be unfavorable in daily life. In extreme cases stress can lead to mental illness. [11]

- Stress has been called the "Health Epidemic of the 21st Century" by the World Health Organization.

*It's time to put the power of positive thought, now understood as the placebo effect, to work for us!*

# Chapter 6

## PUTTING THE PIECES TOGETHER AGAIN

My life was like an under-used and under-appreciated kaleidoscope. It sat on the shelf with the unchanged, existing picture (story) I had created of my life – the image I saw of myself when I first looked through it. I had set out to become a practicing veterinarian and succeeded. It was a familiar image with shadows and colors, both dark and light. Perhaps leaning more to the dark than the light, really. There was comfort, though, in the familiarity I saw as I looked through that kaleidoscope of life without jostling it. As long as my life was in this steady, familiar place, I thought I was fine.

One day, like an earthquake, something jostled my kaleidoscope, turning it all around and upside down. The unexpected car accident and resultant chronic pain syndrome changed everything as I knew it. I watched helplessly as that familiar picture I had known for years fractured into tiny pieces. A crashing mess of shards falling all around, never to be fixed back into that original image I had been so attached to. It was shocking to see life as I knew it shatter. How was I supposed to put all of those moving pieces back in order? How could I ever make it look like the familiar picture I had previously viewed as my life? There was no way I could make it go back to the way it was; back into the familiar parameters of the kaleidoscope image of my life that I knew. Too many pieces had been moved around. I felt as if my life was broken. Shattered.

My kaleidoscope had been sitting in one place gathering dust, displaying the same familiar pattern for a very long time. Yet, I had failed to consider what makes a kaleidoscope – and life – so special. When a Kaleidoscope creates one of its pictures, it does so by moving broken shards and irregular pieces through a messy stage that eventually develops into a beautiful new picture. It takes those broken pieces through chaos before they evolve into the new pattern we experience.

Like the pretty pictures inside a kaleidoscope, our lives are made up of many irregular, smooth, rough, and broken pieces that we fit together into the big picture we perceive as our life. Sometimes we like what we see as our life picture; sometimes we don't. Often, we choose to keep it the same simply because of the comfort found in familiarity, rather than because we like the picture inside the kaleidoscope of our life.

In my case, the turning of my kaleidoscope was involuntary and occurred through tragedy. Tragedy that I later understood was a blessing in disguise. Or, as a friend of mine says, a gift in ugly wrapping. I had been stuck in my beliefs and way of thinking so firmly that I was unable to see the need for and benefits of choosing to turn my kaleidoscope in a new direction. Of creating a new picture for my life. One that was lighter and brighter. I began to understand that my life truly needed to change.

Just as we can take positive action to change an undesirable picture in the kaleidoscope, we have the option to take positive action in our own life, turning it in a new direction to create a more desirable picture or story. We don't have to wait for tragedy to strike. We can take positive action ***now!***

*Intentional change happens in your mind before it happens in your life.*

Initially, as in the hero's journey, where the hero fears and resists change, we may think we want to hang on to our old, familiar story. I certainly did. We may even feel trapped. Betrayed by life. Afraid to adapt to changes thrust on us. I frequently found fear of the unknown or new situations paralyzing. But if we follow the hero's journey format, when we face our greatest fears with willingness and an open mind, we find the courage to take action and turn the kaleidoscope again. We watch as chaos, disappointment, and dissatisfaction evolve into a more joyful life.

Life is dynamic. It moves. Just like the pieces inside a kaleidoscope are meant to move to show their beauty, your life picture will always change and shift as the pieces move around. Don't be afraid to embrace the chaos. It lets you know growth is coming so you can move into a new life picture that you like. One that suits you.

The image developing in the kaleidoscope of my life is beautiful now. And as it continues to turn regularly, I have learned to enjoy each of the new pictures that form, knowing I have the freedom and ability to turn it again if it lands in a picture I don't care for.

Often learning to turn the kaleidoscope – rearranging the broken, dysfunctional pieces of your life in a positive way – involves seeking a mentor or coach who can guide you through the process. Someone who can shorten the learning curve by helping you avoid certain pitfalls and help you see possibilities that you may have missed. Someone who can guide you to new perceptions.

My desire for a better quality of life resulted in my search for help and guidance. Eventually, after years of training and working with mentors and coaches, I realized that my perceptions and how I *choose to respond* to stressors in my life matters more than the stressors themselves. How I choose to respond to negative (or even positive) situations or people around me is actually within my control and directly impacts stress levels. I was so moved by what I learned that I chose to move into hypnosis and coaching as my new full-time career. I experienced such amazing results that it became important for me to share these tools with others.

Again, my intention is that this book will show you that even in the darkest moments there is hope. I found hope, and I will share with you some techniques I've used successfully to overcome the stress and the belief that my life was hopeless and useless. I will show you how you can learn more and get the help you need to move successfully beyond the darkness.

## Chapter 7

## COMMON CHALLENGES

Why is it that some veterinarians absolutely love and thrive in their career while others find it stressful, difficult, and even painful to endure? It's about perception – how we see our lives and the situations that surround us. Based on our perception of the facts of life in and around us, we then choose our internal and external responses. These perceptions and responses dictate the quality of our lives. The doctor who thrives in medicine is the one with a positive outlook and higher emotional intelligence, and who practices willingness, acceptance, openness, and forgiveness daily. In short, they accept life on life's terms.

This is not to say that happy veterinarians wear rose-colored glasses and live a fairytale life. They don't necessarily like everything that happens to them. In fact, they often have things in their lives that are unkind, unjust, or emotionally or physically painful, and crosses that are seemingly impossible to bear. It is, however, their perception of and response to their situation that creates balance and allows them to weather the natural storms of life. Their real life probably isn't any better than yours. They choose to live with a positive mindset and are able to create healthy boundaries.

Having appropriate boundaries is one step toward improving the quality of your life. Veterinarians are notorious for having a lack of personal boundaries and allowing the intrusion of work into their personal lives. Many veterinarians I work with have shared that because of the long hours they work, they have no personal time for themselves or their families. Even on their day off, the office staff often call and ask questions that either could wait until the next scheduled workday, be asked of the doctor currently on duty, or be answered by reading the medical records for a specific pet. Their breaks, when they get them, are interrupted by calls, walk-ins, staff questions, and more that could wait the few minutes until they are back from their much-needed break.

I was a classic example of no personal boundaries. Even though I set limits, I frequently allowed others to breach them. Everyone else's perceived emergencies became my emergencies. I would often find out later that it was an "emergency" to get their pet seen right away not because the pet was having a true medical emergency, but because the client had another engagement that was more fun or "important" to attend at the available appointment times. Other people's lack of planning often became an "emergency" situation I was expected to resolve. When a client didn't want to take time off of work to bring in their pet, I was expected to (and often did) informally extend my work hours to accommodate them.

Heaven forbid we should inconvenience a client, but how often do we let clients inconvenience us, our staff, and our work?

Remember when I had pneumonia and the hospital I worked in was short staffed, so I felt compelled to go back too soon? I believed it was better to inconvenience myself than to inconvenience others, even when it became unhealthy and potentially life-threatening to me.

Veterinarians tend to allow every potential crisis – or what others perceive as a crisis – to become a crisis for them in the moment. They are frequently interrupted with things that really could wait until they finish doing what was truly important at that moment.

This was my habit until I finally understood that I cannot save everyone. Heck, I can't even help everyone! As hard as it was to see others struggle, I learned that there are times when it truly is better to let them work their own way through the situation than to step in and try to "fix" everything for them.

Allowing others to use the power of their own mind to discover viable solutions is actually a courtesy I had robbed many of. It was not only a disservice to them, it was a disservice to me, my time, my quality of life, and sometimes the quality of care I offered because of the distractions I allowed. Yes, there were plenty of times I had to close my eyes, hold my breath, or use some other distraction, praying things worked out well. But in the long run, the vast majority benefited from my enforcing realistic, healthy boundaries.

Many of the veterinarians I have worked with give their cell phone number to clients so they can be reached in case of an "emergency." Then they get frustrated when clients encroach on their personal time by calling at all hours of the day and night for simple, non-emergency questions that should have waited for the next business day. Clients often say they didn't think the doctor would pick up at that hour! They call at midnight because they just remembered that they didn't make an appointment for Fluffy. They expect to leave a message for the next day and are surprised when the doctor answers the number they were given for "emergencies." Or the client may say, "Hey doc, I have a busy day tomorrow, so I won't be able to call during your regular business hours. Will you just answer this quick question for me now?"

This leads to living life in emergency mode, which is highly stressful and unhealthy. Your mind and body never get to relax and recharge, as every ring of the phone automatically triggers the fight or flight response in the body because it is a potential emergency. The body stays in emergency mode for extended periods of time, causing chronic stress and the negative side effects brought on by that. Your conscious mind isn't aware of the constant stress mode, but your body is. It keeps track so that your conscious mind can focus elsewhere. Thus, chronic stress sneaks up on you. For a refresher, review the notes on chronic stress above!

Another challenge stressed doctors face presents as misguided beliefs about what others think about us. We may begin to believe we are not living up to the expectations of others. Maybe we just aren't good enough. Doubt begins to undermine our trust and faith in ourselves as well as our judgment. Our beliefs are challenged. We may focus on what others think about what we are doing rather than the reality that is in front of us – what we know to be the correct thing to do at that moment.

All of this can add up to a sense of overwhelm, doubting your own abilities, even potentially doubting your career choice. Some consider leaving the field they used to love, which then adds guilt to the mixture. They may think, "What if I took someone else's seat in school who might have been better than I am?" Oh, the stories we tell ourselves.

Veterinarians also have the tendency to place very unrealistic expectations of perfectionism on themselves, which leads to guilt, anxiety, and depression. Self-criticism in these perfectionists (read "control freaks") is often brutal. Catastrophizing – always seeing the worst-case scenario as the inevitable outcome – is commonplace. Negative stories are concocted within the imagination.

But what if it's possible to create a different story? What if while you're imagining the worst-case scenario, you could also imagine a best-case scenario? In fact, what if *instead of* imagining the worst-case scenario at all, you automatically choose to imagine the best-case scenario in any given situation? That doesn't mean you don't examine and even prepare for other possible outcomes as your job requires. It also doesn't mean you tell a client presenting a case that is unlikely to turn out well that everything will be fine. It simply means you start with a positive frame of mind and move forward accordingly. It's not about becoming delusional or a Pollyanna; you are learning to approach life from a more positive, compassionate place.

You create the stories you tell yourself in your own mind. If you can generate a negative story, you can generate a positive story. It's your choice. It's your mind. What do you choose to feed or tell your mind?

# Chapter 8

## FEEDING THE HEALTHY MIND

### – THE IMPORTANCE OF UNDERSTANDING BASIC BELIEFS, PERSONAL NEEDS AND CORE VALUES

Our stories, especially the ones we tell ourselves about ourselves, often arise from our inner beliefs and are fed by our perception of the world around us. Dictionary.com defines beliefs as:

1. an acceptance that a statement is true or that something exists.

2. trust, faith, or confidence in someone or something.

Another way to define a belief is as something you hear or say to yourself over and over. Beliefs are often created by simple repetition until it becomes a part of you. The more often you tell yourself something, the sooner you will incorporate it as part of your belief system.

Our early beliefs are typically laid down by our parents and family based on experience and what was important to them. They teach what they believe will serve us best in our life. In many cases, they trained us based on the world that existed for them but no longer exists in that form for us.

If it turns out later that their beliefs and values ultimately don't match what are inherently ours, it's easy to believe that there must be something wrong with us, when, in fact, we are simply our own unique individual. Not wrong. Just different.

What if, as adults, we are able to see our parents and other mentors as perfectly imperfect human beings who do the best they can with the information and tools they have at that moment? What if we choose to see ourselves in that same light? Again, perfectly imperfect. Not wrong, just uniquely, individually us, working with the information and tools we have in the moment.

Personal needs and core values are important drivers in our lives. Often, these terms are used interchangeably. But for discussion here, I am separating them. Basic personal needs, as I use them, is the broader, overriding category. They are applicable to everyone. Core values are narrower, and not all values apply to everyone.

There are five basic personal needs for all people. They are pervasive through our personality. Each individual has their own combination of these; the order and degree of importance can vary widely between individuals. These five needs are

- freedom (flexibility, opportunity),
- security (safety),
- belonging (love, acceptance, connection),
- competency (respect), and

- self-expression (creativity, individualism).

In 2018 I conducted a poll of veterinarians. 281 doctors from all areas of the United States responded. When asked which of these personal needs was most important to them, 46% chose freedom, followed by competency. The rest were spread between the other choices. Curiously, only 0.4% of the responders selected self-expression as their most important personal need. 65% of the respondents chose competency as their second most important personal need. I did not find this result at all surprising, since in order to become a veterinarian, we are required to prove that we are competent – first to be accepted into veterinary medical school, and then into practice.

Why is it important to understand these basic needs and how they color each person's perception of life? Why is it important to honor the differences? It's simple, really. Once you understand the basic human needs and begin to see how they drive you and others around you, it becomes clear why different people perceive the same situation in different ways. As you develop your skill in observing how your perceptions and those of others are driven by these basic needs, it becomes easier to appreciate how misunderstandings occur. When you look at situations with friends, family, coworkers, or clients from this perspective, it is easier to communicate your thoughts in a manner that resonates with them. You can speak from your basic needs position to their basic needs, regardless of how different they are, which allows you to be heard and understood more easily.

In my case, the need to prove my competency began at a very young age and was reinforced year after year, in school and outside of it. Flash back again to the tonsils lesson where I learned the importance of being "good" so I would be rewarded. Proving my competency was simply expected in my family. So naturally, I thought competency should be my primary personal need. It never occurred to me to consider anything different. I lived my life from the perspective of proving my competence and assumed that this was everyone's primary need. After all, if you're not competent, how are you supposed to survive and thrive? In my mind, I was sure everyone wanted to be considered the best at what they did. I was often flummoxed when someone had different priorities. I just couldn't imagine it!

However, when I answered the survey questions for myself, I discovered that freedom was my most important personal need, with competency a runner up. I was surprised at that. Looking back on my life, I can now see how not understanding my true primary personal need had a negative impact on me. All those years, I was trying to fit myself into a box that others had created for me while ignoring my inherent needs. No wonder I spent so much time feeling lost and confused!

Here is a link to download the free survey:

https://brightpaths.lpages.co/personal-needs

You are welcome to take it for yourself to gain deeper insight into your personal basic needs. Be sure to answer based on how you truly feel, not how you think you should feel.

So how might this insight impact you? Let's say, for example, that your parents have security and belonging as their top two personal needs. However, your highest personal needs are freedom and competency. Your parents see rules as a safe framework to work within. They would choose the "safe bet" while avoiding anything that threatens their safety or sense of belonging.

You, on the other hand, are more of a free thinker. You are innovative and want to think outside the box. In fact, why does the darned box have to have such solid sides, anyway? Rules often feel restrictive to you rather than safe. You want to expand your horizons – see what's on the other side of the box's walls. You want to explore new ways of doing things. It is important to you to be free to make your own choices and yet be perceived as competent in what you choose to do in your life.

To your parents who prefer safety, you might be perceived as a risk-taker. Someone who doesn't consider the consequences of your actions. Someone they lost control of and can't understand how or why that happened. They fear for you and your choices. For your future. Yet, you know down deep in your bones, that if you were to play by their rules, you would feel stifled, smothered, trapped, boxed in. Restless and never satisfied. The order of your basic needs is very different than those of your parents. It's not that you want to be unsafe or that you don't want a sense of belonging; you simply want to be free to live your style of life. Safety and belonging are lower priorities for you. You are willing to accept the consequences of your choices as well as the joy of your successes.

That fear or disapproval you perceive from your parents, their attempts to direct you back to the "right" path – their way of thinking – can make you feel like there is something wrong with you. You don't fit the mold they created for you. You sense their spoken or unspoken disappointment in you and your choices. You might feel you are not appreciated for who you are or for the gifts you have to offer. That can create conflict within you that may interfere with your life. Should you make yourself into your parents' idea of what your life should be, or do you pursue your passions?

In my case, early in my life and career, I tried to fit myself into the template my family had carved out for me. A life that would make them proud. Yet, I struggled, wondering what was wrong with me that I didn't feel comfortable and fit into the life I had been so carefully groomed for. I knew all the moves, all the correct things to do. But they always felt like someone else's moves, not my own.

The life I eventually chose is quite different from the one they imagined for me. However, it is a much happier life than the one I had while I tried to follow their perception of what my life should be. My parents came to accept the life I chose and to see that I fit here much better than I ever could have in the one they imagined for me.

It is critical that you honor the real you rather than trying to be what others think you "should" be. Stop trying to fit into someone else's concept of "your" box. You never will fit quite right.

Understanding these basic personal needs reinforces the fact that you are uniquely you and your parents, mentors, friends, coworkers, or children are uniquely them. Neither is "wrong." Each is just different. Trying to fit into someone else's structure or asking others to fit into your structure is begging for frustration and disappointment. No one can do you as well as you can. No one else has the special combination of gifts you bring to the table of life, whether you are able to see them at the moment or not. Conversely, you will not have the special combination of gifts someone else has to offer. That's fine. In fact, that's perfect. It's why there is so much diversity in the world. No one person can do it all. We need each other's uniqueness for the world to thrive.

Why fit in when you were born to stand out? Or, taking it a step further, why even *try* to fit in when you were born to stand out? Thank heavens you are uniquely you. You are needed in this world to fill in where others don't have your unique skills and perspective.

To quote Dr. Seuss from his book *Happy Birthday to You!*,

Today you are You!

That is truer than true!

There is no one alive who is you-er than you!

As you grow in your career and personal life, it is also important to understand your personal or core values, passions, and goals in life. These are different from the basic personal needs discussed above. There is a long list of core values, and unlike the five basic needs we all have, not everyone has all of the core values.

The combination of basic needs and core values creates the unique individual that is you. As you begin to understand and utilize your personal needs and values, you can use that knowledge to guide your behavior and to live a more fulfilling and meaningful life.

Understanding your needs and values gives you a new way of responding to yourself and others. Instead of thinking that there is something wrong with you, you can recognize that your basic needs and values simply have a different order of priority than those of others. While others still have the same needs, they may place a different order of importance to them. Their core values, on the other hand, may be completely different from yours.

You can have compassion for others once you realize that their needs or core values are possibly not being met. This gives you the opportunity to shift the way you address them with the goal of communicating more effectively.

With this understanding, you can also develop compassion for yourself in the times that your needs are not being met. You can then get out of your own way and start to take responsibility for having your needs met in a more consistent and healthy way.

Basic needs and core values drive your decisions and motivate you. They give you a solid framework to guide your decisions, actions, and choices in a way that aligns with your desired life. When you know your needs and core values, you can then ask yourself these questions before you make any decision, choice or take any action:

- Will this decision, choice, or action keep me aligned with my core values?
- Will this decision, choice, or action support my needs?
- Will this decision, choice, or action take me closer to my desired life?

If you cannot answer each of these questions in the affirmative, review the situation and see how you might adjust it so that you do stay in alignment. If it cannot be adjusted, then perhaps the best choice is to pass on the situation in favor of something else that will support you.

Here are some examples of personal core values to guide you in determining yours. This is not an exhaustive list by any means – only a selection to get you started. Pick three to five of these values (or one that is not on this list) to focus on at any given time. Choosing too many will create confusion and overload, stalling your progress. Once you get comfortable with using your three to five values as a guideline in your decision making, you can always expand. Also, with time, you may find that your personal core values shift and change. Life itself shifts and changes. It is important to be flexible.

## A Sampling of Personal Values:

| | | |
|---|---|---|
| Authenticity | Achievement | Adventure |
| Authority | Autonomy | Balance |
| Beauty | Boldness | Compassion |
| Challenge | Community | Competency |
| Contribution | Creativity | Curiosity |
| Fairness | Faith | Family |
| Friendships | Fun | Growth |
| Happiness | Honesty | Humor |
| Influence | Justice | Kindness |
| Knowledge | Leadership | Learning |
| Love | Loyalty | Meaningful Work |
| Openness | Optimism | Peace |
| Pleasure | Poise | Popularity |

| Recognition | Reputation | Respect |
|---|---|---|
| Responsibility | Security | Self-Respect |
| Success | Trustworthiness | Wealth |

When you are single, your personal values will often be quite different than when you are married, when children enter your life, or when you grow and mature in general. I can certainly say that my personal values when I first went into practice were significantly different than they are at this stage of my life. It's a natural part of life to have these values change and grow with you. Start small and simple, and then patiently grow and change. Small changes made regularly create the most effective and sustainable results.

# Chapter 9

## CHANGING THE OLD STORY

The most important lesson I've learned along the way is that change is a process, not a quickie in the back room. It requires patience and tenacity. Openness and willingness. A desire to be in a better place than I am right now. To be a better person than I was in the past. To change my story – both the stories I tell myself and those I tell others.

At first, I thought that changing my story meant that I wasn't a good person in the past. Maybe I was even "bad." That maybe I should be ashamed of who I was then, and now I had to become a "new good person." Maybe in this new story, I should hide who I was before. Tell only the good parts. Then I was afraid that I would lose "me" in the process. Or lose pieces of me. Which one was the real me, anyway?

I eventually learned that all of me is to be treasured. It was that "old me" with all of her good and bad, flaws and choices, that brought me to this place of change, acceptance, and joy. Without the past choices she made, I wouldn't be where I am now. I have learned to love that "old me." To fully embrace every part of myself, warts and all.

My past was not pretty in many places, and it turns out, that's okay. I now realize that every step along the way has been essential to help me arrive at where I am today. In the past, the "old me" was a very unhappy person. I would say things to myself that I would never allow someone else to say to me. Things I would never dream of saying to someone else. I didn't realize I was my own worst critic. My own worst enemy. My tendency was to hang onto the negative things I'd thought, said, or done, reinforcing my earlier training and beliefs that I wasn't good enough. I was like a very possessive dog with a bone, refusing to let go of the bad image I had of myself. Giving myself credit for the good things I did felt unnatural and uncomfortable. There was so much I thought I had to hide.

Back then, I saw life as happening to me rather than something I could participate in. When bad things happened, the world was out to get me. Constantly pushing me down when I was trying so hard to rise up and do good things.

I was sure my life was harder than everyone else's. Certainly, it was much harder than that of those around me who seemed happy. If they knew what was going on, they would understand that the life I had been handed – the circumstances I faced – were tough! They might even feel a little sorry for me. They would want to help, and not make it worse with their own needs and demands. Couldn't anyone see how hard I was trying?

As I mentioned earlier, I sank into significant depression, believing that my life was worthless. It was too hard to live this way. I became one of the statistics who not only considered suicide as a viable option, but also abused alcohol in an effort to change how I felt. Needless to say, it did change how I felt; however, it was far from the improvement I sought. In fact, alcohol reinforced my feelings of uselessness. Like all mind-altering drugs can, alcohol drove me even deeper into despair rather than relieving the stress I went to it for. Freedom from my problems was as elusive as ever. Eventually, I felt even more trapped by the circumstances of my life.

Thanks to the gift of hypnosis, my desire for a different way of life, and my choice to do relentless research to learn how and why some people were happy and I wasn't, I have grown into the happy person I am today. For me, it is a combination of lessons and techniques that work. *No one single modality is the magic bullet.* Through training, trial and error, research, more research, and more willingness to try and fail and try again, I am now able to draw on a wide variety of techniques that have been proven to work through customization to each individual situation. I have also been blessed to help many others across the U.S. and in other countries because of the life I now embrace.

Like everyone, I'm a work in progress. When I adopted the attitude of willingness, acceptance, openness, and forgiveness, I noticed dramatic positive change within and around me.

Willingness to consider that others may have different approaches to life that work. Willingness to see my life and the world around me in a different, more positive light. Willingness to learn and understand why others seem to be happy in their careers and life while I struggled. Willingness to accept that I am not perfect, nor will I ever be. *Willingness to identify and let go of things that no longer serve me.* It took me a while to identify and let go of my old, self-inflicted, self-damaging beliefs and perceptions that wreaked so much havoc in my life.

Acceptance of the facts of life. Acceptance that I am different than others, that others are different from me, and that my concept of right and wrong was skewed and rigid. Acceptance that right and wrong is based on more than just my perceptions and understanding. When I accepted what was real, rather than fighting everyone and everything in the futile effort to make life the way I thought it should be, my stress levels dropped immediately. I discovered that my life was so hard because of my perceptions. My judgmental approach to things. The facts of my life were still real, but how I viewed and lived them was my choice. Once I accepted the facts of life, my suffering ended so that I could begin *living* life. Is there still pain in my life? Yes. But while pain is inevitable, suffering is optional.

Openness to explore new perspectives in life.

Forgiveness didn't mean I had to accept or agree with what offended me, or who I had offended. It meant that I could let go of the relentless suffering that it caused. The hardest part was realizing that the person I needed to forgive the most was myself. I found it difficult to accept that I wasn't perfect. That my thoughts were less than pure at times. That I had made bad choices in life. Over time, I found it was much easier to forgive others for their transgressions, be they real or simply imagined by me, than it was to forgive myself for even the most minor transgressions. Questions like, "Why did I eat that second piece of chocolate" could have me in a tailspin for days…

My bigger transgressions, of which there were many, seemed impossible to forgive. But when I looked at those things through my new perspective, I discovered that forgiving myself didn't mean that those things were suddenly okay to have done; it meant that I could look back and accept that those things were done, learn from them, and move forward in strength without the suffering. Move forward in loving kindness for myself and others. Accept and appreciate what is, rather than fighting to create what I think it should be or should have been.

I've been through quite a few iterations of myself in this life. Some significantly "better" than others. Forgiving the previous iterations of myself that simply didn't know better, or, in some cases, knew better but didn't have the courage to change has been a big factor in my journey. Sometimes, I didn't have the experience or skills needed to make the changes I wanted.

Sometimes the stubbornness of needing to be "right" held me back.

Forgiving everything that led to my challenging childhood was a good start. Yes, my childhood was challenging. Better than some, worse than others. As is the case for most, my childhood experiences guided the formation of my early beliefs and the sense of who I was. In my case, my childhood led me to create and believe the story that I was never quite good enough and never could be. I certainly heard variations on that theme often enough while growing up. As a child, I was told I shouldn't let anyone outside the house see the real me. We were an "upwardly mobile" family, so we had to be sure no one knew where we came from or we wouldn't be accepted. It was vitally important to hide who I really was to gain acceptance in this world.

My beliefs that developed from those childhood stories told me I wasn't good enough and never could be. Those stories limited my progress for years simply because I believed them. Because I allowed them to color my daily living. My subconscious constantly looked for proof to support the belief that I wasn't good enough, though in my conscious mind I thought I was looking for ways to prove to myself and others that I was good enough just the way I was. Of course, since what you believe and focus on comes to be, I was easily able to find proof that I wasn't good enough. It was always right there and available for me to see.

Then there were the choices I've made over the years. Fortunately, I've made some very good choices, but man... What about those others? Some of them were real doozies. Things that I hope no one finds out about. Things I'm grateful that my parents never found out about. Choices that hurt others. Choices that hurt me. I'm sure I harmed people that I never meant to and never realized I had.

I have made some horrible decisions in my past. The longer I lived, the more bad choices I felt I had to hide. The more I had to hide, the worse my past became in my mind. The stories I focused on further supported the belief that I had to hide who I was and where I came from.

And then the second guessing, the Monday-morning-quarterbacking I've done… It is amazing how quickly I can pick apart my actions with thoughts like, "If only I'd thought of that sooner. How could I have missed that sign when it's so obvious now with 20/20 hindsight? Why did I say that? What was I thinking when I did that? My intentions were good; why couldn't she just understand that?"

If my actions harmed someone, I would beat myself up for hours, days, and in many cases years on end. I remember one situation when I was in elementary school that, looking back later, bothered me for years. There was a boy who rode the same bus as I did from the same stop. He said something one day that offended me. My response was to get all elementary-school huffy and blurt out that I was never going to speak to him again.

As time went on, I was really proud of myself for not breaking down and talking to him, even though he tried and tried to get me to talk with him again. I was proud I had stuck to my guns. Then, after a while, I began to wonder why I was doing that, but my pride kept me from talking to him. I eventually started to feel a little sad about it and thought about talking to him. Then, suddenly, he was gone. His family moved away. I never had the opportunity to rectify our relationship.

For years, I thought about that little boy and the impact the situation had on me. How hurt he seemed to be. I regretted not taking action to change things. I regretted that he moved believing I didn't like him, when inside I knew he was a really nice guy – and kind of cute, too. I beat myself up for years over this. My pride had interfered with my apologizing or smoothing over a situation which I had escalated. It took a long time for me to understand that I was just a child then, and it was okay to forgive myself and learn from the incident.

**Lily Tomlin said,**

**"Forgiveness is giving up all hope for a better past."**

I love this statement. It is so freeing. My past is simply my past. Good, bad, or indifferent, it simply was. Acceptance of what is or was has allowed me to learn from the past and move forward with new information, skills, and knowledge. This simple, factual acceptance has allowed me to see that while I didn't necessarily believe it at the time, there has been a lot of good in my life, both in my actions and around me, that benefited myself and others. Of course, there are things about my past that I would change if I could, but since that isn't possible, this level of acceptance has been wonderful, bringing a new brightness to the future. What wonders await me later today or tomorrow?

The old belief of negativity – the world is against me, the only luck I have is bad luck, why should I try so hard when no one will like what I do anyway, I'm always wrong, I'm not good enough and never will be – has been replaced with a new perspective: the universe is conspiring to support me. (Thank you, Michele Gunderson, for your inspired teachings.)

With my eyes open to this new perspective, I began seeing the ways that this was true. As I simply began to accept the possibility that my life could be good, I was gradually able to move from a life of fear and disappointment into a world of comfort and happiness, with frequent forays into actual joy. I rather like where this newest iteration of me is headed.

# Chapter 10

## THE CHANGE PROCESS – HARNESSING THE POWER OF NEUROPLASTICITY

To change your life, you have to start with changing your thought processes, your perceptions. All intentional, desired change happens in the mind before it can happen in your life. By continuing with the current way you think about and approach life, you will continue to perpetuate the things that make you unhappy. By simply changing how you look at things, you can change your future to a happier one. We've heard this from many scholars over the years. They make it sound so simple and easy, but *how* do you do that?

The word "HOW" contains the secret to changing your life. It's in this acronym often used by Alcoholics Anonymous members:

**H** refers to honesty. Being completely honest with yourself allows you to recognize and accept the places where change is important and beneficial.

**O** refers to open-mindedness. A closed mind cannot make change. An open mind allows you see new perspectives and choose which are appropriate to incorporate into your life and which ones you will pass on.

**W** refers to willingness. Being willing to look at new, different perspectives and ideas allows growth. When you are willing to be open-minded and honest, your chances of successfully improving the quality of your life multiply.

In many ways, *it really is that simple.* Change your mind. Manage your thoughts. Choose to live differently. While it may not necessarily be "easy," by understanding some basic facts about your mind and by making regular, small, simple changes, you will experience major results in your life.

Your subconscious mind runs your life. The subconscious mind brings things it believes you should be aware of to the conscious mind based on what it has been trained to acknowledge. How often have you reacted negatively to something without giving it a thought until later, ultimately wishing you had handled the situation better? How often do you find yourself living life on negative autopilot, assuming the worst will happen in any given situation? These are examples of the subconscious mind running your life based on its current, existing programming. By allowing the subconscious mind to run on old beliefs and programs, you will end up with the same old, dissatisfying results.

When you are open to growing and exploring new perspectives, you will likely discover that some of what you thought were your own beliefs are actually the beliefs of others that you have simply accepted at face value as your own. Further exploration may even reveal that your acceptance of these beliefs as your own has taken you down a path that is uncomfortable for you. Not at all suited to your unique self.

What if you could retrain your subconscious to work on a more positive autopilot? To automatically provide you with positive responses, finding the positive in even a challenging situation? What if it really could be that simple? Letting go of the old negative story and replacing it with something kinder? As I have stated, while it may not always be easy, it is that simple.

Your subconscious mind takes what you say to yourself and others literally. The more often you say or think a thought about yourself or your life, the more the subconscious mind believes that thought is very important to you. It believes it is your truth, your reality. Because it runs the show, the subconscious then works very hard to make these important thoughts and beliefs come true for you. **What you focus on expands**. The subconscious will look for ways to support you in whatever thought or belief you focus on. If your thoughts and beliefs are negative, as mine were, then the subconscious will look for ways to support that negativity – to prove you right. This then ingrains the negative thinking even deeper. Your life not only won't improve; it will become progressively more negative.

The brain then becomes rewired to see and acknowledge more of the negative than the positive. This is neuroplasticity in action, but unconscious and often damaging neuroplasticity. The wiring for negative input is strengthened, while the neurons that normally fire when pleasure or positive situations are experienced become quiescent and harder to trigger.

## THE RETICULAR ACTIVATING SYSTEM (RAS)

The key to changing your life is accessing and reprogramming your subconscious mind for success. To institute intentional, self-directed, positive neuroplasticity. As I've said earlier, it's a process of creating change in your mind so that you can successfully change your life. To do this, it's important that you understand the Reticular Activating System (RAS) of your brain.

The reticular activating system (RAS) is a network of neurons located in the brain stem.[12] It has many functions, but the portion of the RAS we will focus on for the purposes of this discussion is that involved in mediating behavior.

In addition to regulating several different functions of the body, a significant job of the RAS is to filter out unnecessary information so that important information can get through to your conscious mind. It determines what filters to create based on what you focus on. It programs itself through neuroplasticity and filters what it allows to the conscious mind based on what you regularly focus on. The RAS filters out what it believes is "junk mail" to bring you only what it perceives as important. That is, what you tend to focus on the most. However, just like the "junk mail" filter on your email, the RAS will inadvertently filter out some good, important information because of its programming.

Just like the oil filter in your car can become clogged with debris, the filters created by the RAS can become clogged with unhelpful information and require changing. When the oil filter of your car is changed, the good oil flows through to where it is needed more easily, keeping the car running at its peak. If that dirty filter is ignored, your car becomes reluctant to start and struggles to keep running. This routine maintenance prevents short- and long-term damage to the car engine.

Similarly, when the RAS filters are clogged with negative thinking, the good parts of life must work extra hard to push through to your conscious mind – if they can get through at all. When the filters created by the RAS remain clogged by the negative, the constant struggle to get healthy thoughts and events through to the conscious mind can be overwhelming, even feeling futile and eventually damaging the mind. Unlike your car, we don't have gauges and lights to tell us when our filters need changing or updating. However, as a car becomes reluctant to start and struggles to keep running on clogged filters, we find ourselves struggling harder and harder to start and get through each day. It's time for a change.

It is entirely possible to reprogram your subconscious mind to perceive and live life differently. To change the negative filters your RAS has been using. You change the old, unhelpful filters, beliefs, and programs of your subconscious by overriding them with positive programs that benefit you. Flushing out the negative thoughts and replacing them with the positive. This is intentional, self-directed neuroplasticity.

It is important to value these old beliefs and programs, as they served a purpose at one time. Often, they were integral to your very survival. However, as you grow and life changes, some of these programs no longer serve you and can hold you back. Honor them for successfully getting you to where you are now and then let them go, replacing them with new beliefs and programs that serve you well today. See *Chapter 24* for simple suggestions to get started immediately.

Circling back to how the filters in the RAS work, it's important to understand that we are constantly bombarded by information. Much more than our conscious mind is capable of taking in or dealing with. An abundance of both negative information and positive information surrounds us at any given moment. Life is designed to be a balance of both positive and negative. Without the negative, we would be unable to see or appreciate the positive in our lives.

Current research suggests that there are approximately eleven million bits of information per second bombarding us from the environment. This information includes things we see, hear, smell, feel, sense, and more. However, we are only able to process fewer than fifty bits per second (this number fluctuates depending on which research model you follow). That means that we are not able to register a lot of information that is available to us. Information that never reaches our conscious mind. This is lucky for us, because if we tried to process all of the information surrounding us at any given time, it would be overwhelming.

Imagine being at a large conference and suddenly everyone – hundreds and hundreds of people – begin talking directly to you at exactly the same moment on completely unrelated subjects, all expecting an immediate, appropriate, and accurate response. Remember the old saying "like drinking from a fire hose?" The information would be difficult to process with any accuracy. The RAS protects you from constant overload and overwhelm. It acts as a gatekeeper for the conscious mind by filtering out unimportant things and only allowing through information that it perceives as important or interesting to you.

It's a pretty efficient system, really. Why should you be burdened by the plethora of irrelevant information? The RAS helps you to focus on what it perceives as important to your life and eliminates distractions. (Squirrel!!!)

Why is it that some people register mostly the negative information, while others register more of the positive information? This relates back to the previous question of why some veterinarians thrive in practice while others struggle.

Let's look at this question from a different angle. Say, for example, that you decide to get a new puppy. You do your research and pick the breed you want, finding that perfect puppy for you and your family. Then, you begin to notice more of the same type of dog around. You see them at the park, on a walk in your neighborhood, on commercials. You notice others talking about the same breed. It seems like they are everywhere now that you have one. You hadn't known that there were so many of these dogs in your town! Did everyone suddenly run out and buy one once you made your decision? Why do you see so many of them now?

In reality, they were there all along. But because you were not previously interested in them, your RAS didn't perceive them as important. It filtered them out before they got to your conscious mind as a distraction. Now that you have expressed interest in this breed, your RAS recognizes it as an important subject, so it stops filtering out that information and allows your conscious mind to become aware of them.

The filters have changed.

This same process occurs when you see more negative things in life than positive. Because you have shown your subconscious and RAS that negative information is more important to you than positive information, it filters out the positive, allowing you to focus your energy on the negative things in life. The things you might perceive as threats.

# Chapter 11

# The LEGACY OF SURVIVAL INSTINCTS

To a certain degree, seeing the negative more easily is hardwired into you. It is part of your natural survival instinct. In order to survive, you need to be aware of potential threats – negative things.

One thing I know about you specifically, whether we have met or not, is that you come from a long line of ancestors who had strong survival instincts. Their good perception and awareness of negative, potentially threatening situations kept them alive. How do I know that? Because you are here; you exist. If your ancestors did not have a strong survival instinct, if they were not aware of the negative around them, they wouldn't have survived to create the lineage that resulted in you. This suggests your natural survival instinct is also strong.

Let's look at what that survival instinct was like in your ancestors. Back in the caveman days, your ancestors had to be on the lookout for negative things that might be threats to their lives such as saber-toothed tigers (okay… I understand that there is some controversy about whether saber-toothed tigers roamed the earth at the same time as man, but hey… this is my story). Let's say one of your ancestors was out hunting or gathering food. Perhaps their survival instincts weren't that strong; they were more laid back and didn't notice potential threats, so they didn't notice that tiger stalking them. They would likely become dinner, and boom, there go your chances of ever being born.

However, your particular ancestors had good survival instincts. Their threat awareness and responses were strong. He or she spotted threats or potential danger more easily and in time. In that moment, their body produced a rush of adrenalin, the stress response, which revved up all kinds of systems in the mind and body and gave them the energy or power burst they needed to escape or fight. To survive. Producing that rush of adrenalin in the face of a threat is the natural stress response of the body. A pretty good thing for them to have, since it meant they survived so you could be here. And, in the process of fighting or running away and escaping, they burned off the excess adrenalin they dumped into their system, which released the stress response state they had entered.

This awareness of the negative served your ancestors well, generation after generation. They survived to pass that strong survival instinct or stress response on to you.

These days, though, the normal physiological cascade of events in the fight or flight stress response has been disrupted. When we focus heavily on the negative in life, whether real or imagined, our stress response stays constantly triggered, be it on slow simmer or red alert.

You see, our subconscious mind, the one that regulates the fight or flight response, cannot tell the difference between a real or an imagined threat. A potential or even an entirely imagined threat – one made up in your mind – is taken just as seriously by the body as actually seeing that saber-toothed tiger stalking you.

While we don't have to survive encounters with saber-toothed tigers today, when our mind perceives a potential threat, real or imagined, the same fight or flight reaction or stress response is triggered in the body. Unlike our ancestors, who would exert sufficient energy to immediately consume the adrenalin released, thus releasing the stress response, we typically don't have a way to physically burn off the excess adrenalin that is dumped into our body. So it sits there and stews. This creates chronic stress and all of the serious consequences that develop from it.

# Chapter 12

# EFFECTS OF CHRONIC STRESS

For us, the fight or flight survival reaction is more commonly sparked by, say, the boss calling you into the office, or your tech telling you that you're backed up in the lobby with all rooms filled and you have a hit-by-car pet on its way to the back. Or perhaps one of your "favorite" clients with sweet little Fluffy is in the next room waiting to see you. You know... that client/pet combo that keeps you wondering which one is going to take a bite out of you first.

For those of you who freely give your personal number out to your clients, the stress response is also triggered every time your phone rings during your time off, whether it's a true emergency or not, simply because it *might* be an emergency. It sends the same message to your body as spotting that stalking tiger would.

While your natural survival instinct in these cases triggers your body to run or fight, it's not considered appropriate to simply run out of the room or to start a fight with a boss, client, or pet. You are stuck standing there dealing with it, with no way to release the adrenalin stew that is swirling inside and creating an ugly mess of chronic stress.

Stress and anxiety manifest in many ways. A common physical manifestation is high blood pressure. Chronic gastrointestinal (GI) issues are another classic indicator of excess stress. Do you walk around popping antacids like candy? Or have you graduated to prescription medications? I certainly did for a long time. Doctor after doctor tried to figure out why I was having such persistent GI issues. I even underwent major surgery trying to fix the problem. And it didn't.

Never once during all that time did a doctor ask me about my stress or anxiety levels. Nor did anyone make any practical suggestions on how to manage chronic stress in healthy ways.

According to webmd.com, healthline.com, clevelandclinic.org, and numerous other medical resources, chronic stress can cause an individual to experience

- Emotional symptoms such as
    - becoming easily agitated, frustrated and moody;
    - feeling overwhelmed, "out of it", out of control; and
    - decreased self-worth, low self-esteem, loneliness, and isolation.
- Physical symptoms such as
    - decreased energy,
    - headaches,
    - upset stomach and various forms of GI issues,
    - chronic aches and pain,
    - frequent illnesses such as colds, and
    - increased blood pressure and heart rate.
- Cognitive symptoms such as

- excessive worry,
- forgetfulness and disorganization,
- inability to focus,
- increased medical mistakes,
- poor judgment, and
- being pessimistic or seeing only the negative.

- Behavioral symptoms such as
  - changes in appetite;
  - procrastinating and avoiding responsibilities; and
  - inappropriate coping skills such as increased use of alcohol, drugs, cigarettes, gambling and even suicide.

Clevelandclinic.org states, "Stress is linked to 6 of the leading causes of death: heart disease, cancer, lung ailments, accidents, cirrhosis of the liver, and suicide."[13]

What if there were simple yet powerful ways to change your work and personal life from stressed out, overwhelmed, anxiety-ridden, and frustrating to satisfying, creative, fun, rewarding, and passionate? To go from frazzled to dazzled by your life? There are, and I will offer suggestions as we go.

It is important to create safe, effective ways for your mind and body to release excess stress. Practical ways to create down time before you crash. If you don't proactively plan de-stressing activities and break times for yourself, your mind and/or body will simply choose a time to shut down on its own, often at the most inconvenient times.

One simple, practical way to create a more relaxed, satisfying life is to actively cultivate a positive mindset. As noted above, stress often leads to a pessimistic, negative approach to life and vice versa. By actively cultivating a positive mindset, you can significantly decrease your stress levels, which automatically increases your satisfaction in life.

To a substantial degree, we have control over which fifty of those eleven million bits of information per second we receive and process. If we expect to be bombarded with negative information and thoughts consistently, then we train the brain – the RAS – to notice them more than we notice the positive bits of information. When the RAS perceives that you are more interested in or focused on negative things, it filters out the positive around you, allowing you to maintain your conscious focus on what it perceives as the all-important negative. It's not that the positive isn't there around you; it's that your conscious mind isn't given the opportunity see it.

This is undirected neuroplasticity in action – something we just allow to happen when we allow our circumstances to dictate how we feel, respond, or react. When our initial choice is to focus on something negative, we intentionally retrain or rewire our brain to select for it. Then, as more and more negative information is brought to our conscious attention by the RAS, we inadvertently reinforce that negative selection, strengthening those neural pathways even further. So when we give the brain its initial instructions to see something negative, the RAS focuses on supporting what we initially told it: "Look for the negative." After all, our brain is there to protect and serve us, so it feeds us what we ask it to notice. In this case, we are fed a mental diet of the negative information in our environment.

Notice the subtle distinction here. All information – positive, negative, and neutral – is available to us at all times. However, when we show a preference for the negative, the brain then takes that as its cue to build filters. Once we show it what is important to us, the brain then takes off on its own to build strong neural pathways to support that preference.

# Chapter 13

## SHIFTING FOCUS TO THE POSITIVE

However, it's possible to shift our perspective (turn that kaleidoscope) and begin intentionally looking for the positive in those eleven million bits of information per second we are showered with. Just like when you made the conscious decision to pick a specific breed of puppy and suddenly began seeing more of them, the RAS will begin to allow more of the positive bits of information through to your conscious mind. Because we can only process fifty bits of information per second in the conscious mind, the RAS must then filter out more of the negative information in order to make room and allow the positive information through.

As our brains become more accustomed to recognizing the importance of positive information, more supportive information will filter through and be processed than negative. This is intentional or self-directed neuroplasticity, where you direct the brain to rewire itself in a new – in this case, positive, useful – way. The new filters that the RAS creates and uses to provide us with important information will change. Instead of living on negative autopilot, swirling in that adrenalin stew, we begin to live on a more positive autopilot. We begin to enjoy more of life because we now notice there is more out there to enjoy. It's a gradual process that takes time, patience, persistence, practice and, most importantly, a willingness to be open to the positive that surrounds us.

I finally realized that my perception and how I chose to respond to the stressors mattered more than what the stressors in my life were. How I choose to respond to negative situations or people is fully within my control and directly impacts my stress level.

Imagine the difference in how you would feel inside if the world around you appeared more positive!

Remember, positive change requires a willingness to let go of things that no longer serve you. Releasing disempowering thoughts and actions. Learning new ways to see yourself, your work, and life around you.

A big step for me has been learning to let go of my need to get approval from my parents, family, friends, coworkers, or boss. I am learning to find that approval inside myself. This was no easy task! I craved approval from others all my life. I based my self-worth on what others thought about me and my work. My internal belief system was programmed to believe I wasn't any good if others didn't openly and regularly show appreciation for me.

Needless-to-say, I spent my life setting myself up for disappointment. Other people have their own lives and needs, yet I wanted them to be sure to think about and compliment me on what I did. I thought I was doing certain things very well; but at the same time, I was so unsure of myself that I wanted others to notice and acknowledge my accomplishments. My behavior was based on my childhood interpretation of being good when my tonsils were removed and the reward of getting a puppy. I wanted – no, craved – that tangible reward for having done something well.

I didn't realize how externally focused I was and can still be sometimes. How easy it is to get wrapped up in creating a story about others judging me. If I didn't get a puppy, then I must not have been good. In my mind, no one was there to support me. But it sure was easy to find people willing to criticize me.

When others were too busy to notice, or did notice but didn't see the need to compliment me, I assumed I had done something wrong. That my work wasn't good enough to be appreciated. This became very discouraging. Maybe if I worked harder, they would notice and appreciate me more. When that still didn't happen, no matter how hard I worked, it was even more discouraging.

What if I chose to work less? Be less efficient? Well, that certainly *was* noticed and commented on! I felt I couldn't win. The harder I worked, the less appreciated I felt. And if I had an off day or slacked off in the slightest, I was criticized. I must be a pretty bad person if no one saw enough good in me to compliment me for work well done. With all the lack of acknowledgement for my work, I felt even more like an imposter.

# Chapter 14

# THE IMPOSTER SYNDROME

Imposter syndrome – feeling like you are "not good enough" to do the job you are doing – comes in all sizes and shapes across every field. Veterinarians struggling with imposter syndrome do not have a monopoly on it. They are far from alone in their thoughts and imaginings.

Imposter syndrome causes you to subconsciously set yourself up to fail. Your thoughts and feelings of not being good enough block you from being aware of the evidence around you that proves you really are good. Why is it that so many professional adults suffer from the belief that they aren't good enough and will fail if they try to do certain things?

Your imagination is the most powerful life tool you have. Yet, it is often used to deceive yourself with negative self-talk. Stories that are completely untrue or based on little foundation. Things you tell yourself that only you could think up. And often, the stories you feed yourself feel so real! The more you run the imagined negative stories in your head, the more it becomes like quicksand. You become mired in it. You convince yourself of its truth until it becomes a belief that will eventually drag you under. This is another example of neuroplasticity at work – training your RAS what to look for and what to hide from your conscious mind.

However, just as there are ways to safely escape quicksand, there are ways to escape from the negative self-stories we have become mired in.

Elizabeth Gilbert stated it so beautifully in her book *Eat, Pray, Love* when she said, "You need to learn how to select your thoughts just the same way you select your clothes every day. This is a power you can cultivate. If you want to control things in your life so bad, work on the mind. That's the only thing you should be trying to control."

Ahhhh...... positive neuroplasticity at its best.

# Chapter 15

# A POWERFUL TOOL FOR CHANGE

We were out to dinner with our daughter and her family one evening when our eight-year-old grandson got us all thinking by asking a simple question. He said, "Imagine you are alone on a small deserted island. A volcano is about to erupt. What would you do?" After considerable discussion around the table about possible options, my grandson laughed and said, "Stop imagining it!"

I was amazed by the astuteness of this eight-year-old. Here we were, adults and kids alike, clearly overanalyzing the situation, feeling the stress build as we tried to figure out the best solution, and completely missing the obvious answer. Keep it simple. Stop imagining it. We were all creating stories to avoid the potential negative consequences of a story we had conjured up entirely in our own minds. It wasn't even real!

Each of our islands, volcanoes, and situations were created

differently in our minds, even though we all started with the same information. We imagined all sorts of things, possibly drawing on our previous life experience of stressful situations – what tools we had, what our options were, and how likely we were to survive this "dire" situation we imagined ourselves in. The stories we created in our minds were not even based on reality. We created these stories based on an imaginary question someone asked.

What if this had been a casual, or maybe a careless comment – or lack of comment – from a friend, co-worker, boss, partner, or client? Something that may or may not have even been real? What would your imagination do with it? Oh, the stories we tell ourselves. How powerful our imagination is! It can create the most amazing things out of nothing.

Think about the chair you are sitting in right now. The only way it came to be was from someone's imagination. What started as a thought in their imagination became a reality. What reality do you choose to create for yourself?

The stories we create within our mind, our imagination, represent only one possible outcome. If we can generate, create, or imagine one story, what other possible stories might we be able to create? If we can generate a negative story around a given situation, we can generate a positive story.

If I can create a story of being an imposter, I can just as easily use that same information and imagination to create a story that I completely deserve to be where I am. I worked hard for it. I passed the tests. I successfully do my job daily. While I'm not perfect, thank heavens, I am qualified and worthy to be where I am, doing what I do. I am perfectly imperfect.

**Use your imagination to create your own positive story!**

Again, why is it that some veterinarians absolutely love and thrive in their career while others find it stressful, difficult, and even painful to endure? It's about perception. How we see our lives and the situations that surround us. What do you spend time imagining?

*"Experience is not what happens to you – it's how you interpret what happens to you."*

*– Aldous Huxley*

An adaptation of this statement might be: Life is not what happens to you; it's what you make of your personal circumstances.

You have been given life. It's up to you to decide if you will make it a good one or a bad one.

*Stop the World, I Want to get Off* is a musical that illustrates how we are often dissatisfied with the life we have because it didn't turn out exactly how we imagined it. Sometimes only one single portion isn't how we wanted it, and we allow that perceived negative thing to distort our view of life in general. This is beautifully illustrated in the musical by the main character, Littlechap, who wants one thing he doesn't have. Just one thing.

Littlechap has an amazing, loving wife, a job that has made him wealthy, and two daughters. However, he believes that his life is unfair and bad because he never had a son. In the game of life, he has been dealt a bad hand. He received the short stick. As his life evolves, with every challenge he faces, Littlechap freezes the action for a moment, turns, and says to the audience, "Stop the world; I want to get off." In other words, he sees only the negative and the hardships. He keeps wanting to run away, quitting instead of looking for positive solutions. Rather than cultivate the wonders he already has in his life, he chooses the distraction of numerous affairs – searching for something to make him happy – as a substitute for the son he feels cheated out of.

Rather than focusing on the beauty of all he has, things that many people would be over-the-moon with joy to have, he focuses on the one thing he doesn't have. Because of this misplaced focus, he becomes dissatisfied with his entire life. The normal ups and downs which life presents us all are overwhelming to him. He considers them to be more proof of the unjust life he has been given.

Can you see how he programmed his RAS to focus on the negative? He just wants out of his perceived miserable lot in life. "Stop the world, I want to get off." I quit. I'm never going to get what I want.

It isn't until his wife dies that he realizes he's always had the most important things of all – a loving wife and a wonderful life. This truth he finally discovers comes too late for him. He's missed out on enjoying a wonderful life because of his perceptions.

This is often the case for dissatisfied, unhappy people. Many don't ever see the good in their lives, and they die miserable. They quit looking for and seeing the beauty around them, blinded by the negative, regardless of how big or small it is in the overall scheme of life. They quit.

"Stop the world, I want to get off." A metaphor for suicide possibly? Things aren't going the way I want them to, so I'm going to bail. Whether it is the actual physical taking of a life, or by checking out mentally and emotionally, it most certainly is a form of focusing on only the negative parts of life while choosing to ignore the positive aspects of life.

When I look back to the time I contemplated suicide, lying in bed, watching the fan slowly turn and turn, I realize now that I, too, wanted to stop the world and get off because I was so focused on the bad parts of my life: the agonizing death of my boyfriend, the failure that was my first job, my perceived failure at being a practice owner, my failure at being what my parents thought I should be, the car accident that caused the chronic pain syndrome and loss of my career, the failure to have a traditional family like the rest of my family. I could go on and on, as there have been many additional tragic events and losses in my life.

However, I was lucky. Or was I stubborn? Or something else? In my mind, I had more than enough good reasons to allow myself to get tired, worn down, and pushed to the point of quitting altogether. But even at my darkest point, I didn't. Instead, I chose to face another day – just one more day to see if there was any reason out there to keep going. To look for a way to survive.

I finally realized that it was up to me to reach out for help to fulfill my own basic needs. It was not up to someone else to rescue me, to notice that my needs were not being met and step in to "fix" it all for me. I was the only one who could determine the order of my basic needs, decide if they were being met, and know what my personal core values were.

But I didn't know how to figure that out on my own, initially. It was hard to admit that I couldn't make some of the changes I needed on my own. I was an independent woman who had gotten this far in life, only to realize that it was my own "stinking thinking" (as a dear friend likes to call it) that got me into the negative situation I found myself in.

Eventually, after much struggle, a few false starts with counselors and coaches who weren't right for me, and more dark hours, I found *and accepted* outside help from counselors, coaches, and mentors that did work for me. Once I was willing to accept help from others, I learned new coping techniques and skills. I learned that my perspective wasn't the only one. Nor was it the healthiest one. I chose life. To not only survive, but to find a way to thrive. It turned out it wasn't easy, but it was fairly simple. A series of small, simple steps taken day in and day out, consistently.

*I took responsibility for the quality of my life.*

This led me to create a simple, five-step system for change called The Brain System™. I have distilled my years of work down to five steps in a logical system that consistently creates positive change. These are the steps I have taken to create the changes I want in life. They are the steps I walk my clients through to successfully achieve the positive changes they desire in their lives.

The BRAIN System™ stands for:

**B**elieve – that you can make positive change in your life using the power of your own mind.

**R**elease – anything that no longer serves you.

**A**djust – make small, powerful adjustments to get big results.

**I**nstall – new perceptions, beliefs and habits.

**N**europlasticity – enjoy the benefits as you reprogram or rewire your own brain to perceive the positive in life automatically.

I go into detail on how you can implement this simple system to effectively change your life a little later in the book.

# Chapter 16

# PERSISTENCE AND PERCEPTION

When I created and implemented The BRAIN System™ to change the way I encountered life, my stress and stress-related symptoms decreased. I accepted that my ***perception*** of life made life stressful. When I chose to change my perceptions, my life changed.

Don't give up on the wonderful parts that are present in life. Don't let quitting be the choice you make. While you may not be able to see the positive at this moment, it is there when you simply learn how to look for it.

You are a great and worthy cause.

> *"Every great cause is born from repeated failures and from imperfect achievements."*
> – Maria Montessori

When you were young, you tried a lot of new things and failed miserably. The first time you tried to walk across the room to your mommy, you probably only made it one or two steps before you fell. Kaboom! Failure! Thank heavens for those well-padded diapers. You failed in your quest to walk across the room to mommy. But you didn't let that failure stop you. It excited you! You kept getting up and doing it again until you could not only walk, but run, hop, skip, and even dance.

The first time you attempted to ride a two-wheeled bike, you were likely very wobbly and fell a time or two, probably skinning a few knees and elbows while navigating the learning curve. Maybe you scratched the shiny paint on your brand-new bike.

I received stitches in my ankle and a new scar to show off to my friends after one significant wreck. Epic "failure" there. Even after my injury, though, I got back on my bike! I persisted until I became proficient at riding my bike, and I continued to get joy from the accomplishment and freedom associated with it. I still enjoy the wind in my face as I ride in my memories.

You probably had many "failures" at riding a bicycle before you found your balance and rhythm, becoming proficient at it. Yet, like me, you kept practicing on your bike until you got better. It's not that you weren't afraid. After all, it's no fun to fall off a bike, getting scrapes, cuts, and maybe even a few broken bones. Another epic fail! The difference between your younger self and now is that, back then, you were determined to learn that new skill, so you kept practicing. You didn't give up when you had failures – even the epic ones. You kept going, kept practicing.

It is said that winners make the most mistakes because they never quit. They keep practicing, trying over and over, and learning from their mistakes rather than quitting due to them.

*"There is something to be said for keeping at a thing, isn't there?"*

*– Frank Sinatra*

Success doesn't necessarily come from being gifted or above average. It comes from being determined, taking action, practicing, and exploring. Success means learning from your mistakes (formerly known as "failures"), picking yourself up from that perceived "fail" and continuing forward. Success comes from seeing what you might have previously considered a failure as a learning opportunity. Looking at the experience with curiosity rather than with judgment. It's about being determined and persistent in learning a new skill, enduring the occasional skinned knee or bruised pride along the way. Even if that skill is simply how to navigate life effectively. It's about letting go of old beliefs that limit or block you from the success you desire, allowing yourself to see things from a different perspective. Instead of thinking "well, that didn't work.... I quit," consider "well, that didn't work.... what can I learn from this and change to improve future outcomes?"

When you were little and trying out those first steps, even though you technically "failed" at your goal of walking to mommy, you didn't see it as failure. That first brave step excited you, even though it led to the "failure" of falling before you got there. The real success here is that you tried and persisted until you worked it out. You didn't reach your grand goal with that first try, but you were excited, not discouraged. It's all about perception. Your mommy, and everyone else watching you, didn't see falling as a failure; they saw the huge, amazing success of your first step. It's all about perception.

At what point in your life did the excitement of trying something new, failing, getting up, trying again, and eventually developing that new skill turn into trying, failing, and giving up on yourself? At what point did you develop that fear of even trying because you might, potentially, possibly, or even likely fail?

*"No matter how hard you work for success, if your thought is saturated with the fear of failure, it'll kill your efforts, neutralize your endeavors, and make success impossible."*
– Baudjuin

Often, we adults think of something we've done that didn't work out the way we planned as a failure instead of a learning experience or challenge. We forget how brave it was to believe in yourself and take that first step. We assume that the rest of the world sees it (read: you) as a failure too, when, in fact, they don't see failure at all. Some even look at you with admiration that you had the guts (read: belief, determination, desire, or faith) they didn't have to give it a go. Admiration for the effort and how far you did get, even if they don't express it directly to you. It's all about perception. Seeing and acknowledging the successful parts of what you did, rather than the "failure" you perceived that wasn't even a failure. There is always some success in everything we do, even if it's learning what not to do next time! It's all about perception.

*Our greatest glory is not in never falling but in rising every time we fall."*

– Confucius

## Chapter 17

## LISTENING TO YOUR INNER VOICE: HONORING YOUR PERSONAL NEEDS

For much of my life, changing my mind, or not following through on a commitment felt like a failure. If I made a commitment to someone or something, it meant I *had* to follow through or complete it, even if it was not in my best interest to do so. However, I had an experience that led me to a profound understanding of change, perception, and self-care.

I had made a commitment to go to Mexico with a group of people. When I made that commitment, I was excited and looking forward to the trip. I had been to the same location with this group the year before and loved my time there. I came home with the certainty that I was joining them again this year. I couldn't wait.

Yet, as the trip neared, I began to dread it. Nothing had happened or changed. No particular reason for this change in my feelings, just an increasing certainty that I really did not want to go. My inner voice was clearly telling me not to go. But I had made the commitment to them and I always work hard at honoring my commitments. I consider it an important part of myself. I *really* don't like letting people down… to a fault. Not going, in my mind, would have meant I had failed to keep my promise. I was failing at holding up my end of the agreement with them.

When the time came, I went. For the most part, I enjoyed the beginning of my time there, but there was still that nagging feeling that I didn't want to be there. I was in the wrong place. There was someplace else I would be better served. As the week progressed, I became more and more restless. I had a very strong desire to leave, even though my return flight wasn't for several days. Because of the remoteness of the location, changing my plans had the potential to be challenging and costly.

I convinced myself to stay because it was the "right" thing to do. I didn't want to disappoint my friends by not doing my part. I would just make the best of the situation I had gotten myself into by not listening to my inner voice when it clearly said, "Don't go!" I continued to stay at the retreat, even though I knew it was not the right place for me to be.

I held on for another day, but the pull to leave became unbearable the next morning. My inner voice was screaming at me. That voice that I often hear and choose to ignore because I'd made a commitment to someone else.

We make commitments based on the information we have at the time. We use our best judgment and take action. But what if, as we get further into the commitment we discover, as I did, that we've committed to the wrong thing? What if it turns out to be something that doesn't align with our current needs, values, or beliefs?

In the past, I would typically suffer through to the bitter end simply because I had made that commitment. But what if I could recognize my misstep sooner, perhaps by listening to my inner voice, and find a way to gracefully extricate myself in a way that wouldn't cause harm? What if, instead of being the doormat that everyone wiped their feet on because I allowed it, I could honor myself as deeply as I tend to honor my commitments to others?

When an unexpected opportunity to leave presented itself, I took it immediately. Instead of berating myself for "ducking out on my commitment," I seized the opportunity to listen to my higher, wiser mind and body. I realized that this time I needed to listen to and trust that voice. What if, rather than running my old program of sticking it out at my own expense because I had made that damned commitment, I listened to my heart? This time, unlike back when I ignored my inner voice and body when they told me I needed to take time off to recover from pneumonia, I listened.

My stress levels decreased immediately. There was such a freedom and power in making the choice to honor myself and my own needs, instead of staying miserable in a situation I felt stuck in. As the day progressed, I became more and more elated by my choice to honor myself in a way I wouldn't have dared to in the past. For conquering the fear of being looked down on, making someone else unhappy, or being perceived as a quitter. A failure. I honored my inner voice, my personal needs, knowing it was the right choice for me.

And, wonder of wonders, over the next few days, my peers and many of those from the trip shared that they admired me for listening to my inner voice and my body! *They respected my decision for self-care over self-sacrifice!* They didn't perceive my actions as a failure at all! I was so sure my decision would be perceived as selfish. The stories I had created with my own imagination about not wanting to appear selfish had become so ingrained, I was too frightened to listen to my wiser inner voice and body, even when they were screaming at me. Yet when I chose to see things differently and act on what resonated with me in a healthier way, I discovered that those were just stories I had created in my own imagination. Reality was quite different than what I had conjured up in my crazy mind. A perfect example of how I created a story in my own mind that was disempowering. When I chose to change it into a different story, I felt so empowered. So light. So right.

It can be challenging to develop new internal belief systems – new ways to look at yourself and life. While it's important to depend on and believe in yourself, there is a definite need for external support while you learn and establish this new skill. Just like it is important to receive feedback from the training wheels on your bicycle in the beginning, telling you when you stray too far in one direction or another, it is important to have at least one person who is a positive mirror for you. Someone who will reflect back to you the good you may have overlooked, the personal internal strengths it can be easy to forget while living in a challenging world.

Mind you, this isn't just a "yes person" who will agree with anything you say. Someone to pump up your ego while misleading you into believing all of the stories, true or not, that you tell yourself. This is someone who will look at each situation from a grounded, detached position and help you sort through the real and imagined, the good and the bad (and the things you are trying to con yourself with) and remind you of the true good and successes within you without judgment. Again, someone who will act as a mirror for your strengths and progress. Not everyone has someone like this in their life, especially when they are in the early stages of recognizing they wish to make a change.

Often, the people you have inadvertently surrounded yourself with are those who are attracted to your negativism, or negativism in general. People who are perceived as having similar beliefs, leading you into a sense of false comfort or camaraderie. People who might eventually try to sabotage you as they become uncomfortable with your growth and change. It's important to identify those who undermine your progress under the guise of being helpful "for your own good."

Often, a professional mentor or coach is the best option here, especially until your desired changes begin to become your reality. Once your new belief systems are more established, you will begin to attract more positive people to you naturally.

Believing in yourself as the perfectly imperfect individual that you are is a learned skill. A skill that needs to be practiced regularly to become established and maintained. This is not a quick fix without setbacks or frustrations; rather, it requires the sustained persistence that is required to gain any new skill.

Be that baby who falls after one or two steps then excitedly waves their happy fists in the air and gets up to do it again. Be patient with yourself. You are learning a new skill or improving one that is partially developed. Rejoice in the knowledge that you are learning something new.

*"Only those who dare to fail greatly can achieve greatly."*

– Robert F. Kennedy

# Chapter 18

## The BEGINNER'S MIND

One of the most dangerous thoughts you can entertain is, "I already know that." It blocks you from learning new things or seeing the things you think you already know from a different perspective. That willingness and openness to learn is lost, and so is the wonder and joy of seeing new things.

Having the mindset of a beginner is an invaluable trait to cultivate. The beginner's mind is open to learning, even about things you may think you already know. The beginner's mind is open to growth. It is a curious mind. Eager to explore new perspectives and ideas. When you are a beginner, it's accepted that you won't do everything right the first time or possibly even the first umpteen times you try it. In some cases, you may never "get it right," and that's okay, too. We are not meant to do everything. A beginner, by default, has permission to make mistakes. You're new at this and that's not just okay, it's wonderful. Exploring new and old thoughts from a beginner's perspective can be fun!

Mistakes, formerly known as failures, are an accepted part of learning. They are an important part of learning. Think of the professional tennis player who, even though they know their sport inside and out, will continue to practice with a coach. They already know how to execute their skills at an extremely high level, yet they are always willing to learn. Here they are at the top of their game and darned if they don't make a mistake that sends the ball into the net or out of bounds, even at their level of expertise. They learn from that mistake, both by themselves and with the help of their coach reflecting back to them not only what went wrong with that one play, but also all of the things that went so right.

By keeping the mind of a beginner in everyday life, you give yourself the freedom to try, make mistakes, learn, try again, and work your way to success. After all, every day is a new one that you've never lived before. Every day is a new beginning. You are automatically a beginner at the beginning of each day. And you can begin your day over at any point throughout it. Treasure the opportunity to approach life with an open, curious, non-judgmental, beginner's mind.

Everyone starts as a beginner. We become beginners again at various stages in our lives, depending on what we are doing. I became a beginner again at age sixty when I chose to learn new, healthier ways to take care of myself and more joyful ways to approach life.

Initially, it was hard to give myself permission to make mistakes as I tried this beginner mindset. Here I was, at my age, learning new things about life. Things I thought I already knew. Talk about feeling awkward! I had thoughts like, "Good heavens, shouldn't I have learned this before I got to this age?" Why did it take me so long? How could my perception of life have been so skewed? Why did I stubbornly hang on to the perceptions that were not only skewed, but harmful?

By taking on the beginner's mindset, I was able to learn new things about what I thought I already understood. Things that others learned in their teens and twenties. For heaven's sake, I was sixty! Taking on the beginner's mindset at my age felt odd, yet so important.

But I also learned by doing this that *I* wasn't a failure. Did I fail at some things I tried? Sure! But *I* wasn't a failure. It was all about my perceptions. Not everything in life is supposed to be rosy. I'm not supposed to do it all. When I became willing to see myself, my life, my career, family, and friends from a different perspective, things changed for me. Dramatically! It was like another turn of the kaleidoscope. Those broken pieces fell into a new picture when I gave myself a new opportunity with a "better late than never" attitude. I became a beginner in life again. Open. Curious. Non-judgmental. Willing. That word, willing, keeps showing up because it is the basis for all successful change.

I hope you take the opportunity to learn sooner than I did that being a beginner is something that happens daily, in all stages of life. It is something to be embraced and enjoyed. My hope is that by applying this information to your own life, you will be willing to adopt the beginner's mindset approach to life and experience the true freedom and joy it can bring as you work your way to success.

If you are willing to be alive and actually live your life, then open your beginner's mind today.

Notice that I use "work your way to success" rather than saying "getting it right" or "doing it perfectly." That is because the desire or need or drive to do things right or perfectly will ultimately drive you back into self-doubt and down the rabbit hole of despair.

# Chapter 19

## PERFECTION VS. SUCCESS

Perfection is rigid and unforgiving. It either is or isn't, and different people have different perspectives on how perfection should look. So technically, nothing can ever be perfect because not everyone will see it in the same light. Perfection does not necessarily equate to success.

Perhaps your idea of a perfectly decorated entry way or lobby is having everything in the most modern, stainless steel, grey and white motif. Its clean, crisp, no nonsense appearance perfectly depicts the clean, crisp, no nonsense approach you have to your work. Yet, your colleague down the street prefers an antique-appointed lobby with inviting colors that reflect the down-home feel he exudes with his grandfatherly approach to his job. Both individuals are equally competent and excel in their field. Both have designed their perfect work environment to express themselves perfectly, yet neither would be comfortable working in the other's perceived "perfect" workspace. Both are completely different, and yet each is perfect in their creator's mind.

Think, too, about the importance of understanding personal needs. In the previous example, the perfect life for one's parents might include a Monday to Friday nine-to-five job with a weekly, predictable paycheck, a retirement plan, and complete predictability of what they will face every day when they go into the office. They know what is expected of them, what they are supposed to do, and the hours they have in which to complete the day's tasks. No big surprises. They come home to dinner at the same time every day. They have their evening routine with their average 2.54 children, spouse, and one dog. Their weekends are planned out well ahead of time. They feel safe and secure in their perfect life. And… they want that for you. They want you to have their perceived perfect life. After all, it's perfect for them, so why wouldn't it be perfect for you, too?

However, if your primary personal need is freedom, not security, the thought of all that consistency day in and day out makes you shudder. You would feel so trapped in your parents' "perfect" lifestyle. Bored would be an understatement. You want a career where there is challenge, excitement. One where you can make a difference. Where you have flexibility to think in new, creative ways. In the medical field, you never know what's going to walk in the door, and that's fine with you. The variety of life stimulates you. Your income depends on the number and type of appointments that you see. It is rarely consistent, but you have the ability to make choices that affect your revenue.

When you have days off, you want to be free to choose how you spend them. Be spontaneous sometimes. Go out to dinner on short notice with some friends. Drive to another town just to see what is there. Follow up on a lead someone gave you about a fantastic new restaurant, amusement park, camp site, or whatever appeals to you. You may choose to just "veg out" in a quiet place. The freedom of choice is a high priority. That is your perfect life.

The unpredictability of your freedom-based lifestyle would bring anxiety and stress to your parents, who have security as their primary need. And yet, to you, variety is the spice of life. It's perfect.

Success, on the other hand, has latitude. It isn't all or nothing. You can successfully do something that may not be done perfectly. Let's say two different doctors see a pet with the same medical condition: a dog with a broken leg. Assuming for the moment that the fractures are identical and all other parameters are the same, each doctor chooses a technique to use. The first doctor chooses a technique that he is comfortable with – that in his hands has been and will likely again be successful. The second doctor chooses a completely different technique that she is comfortable with. Both outcomes are equally successful. But were they perfect? Likely, each of these doctors would feel that they chose the perfect technique. And in their hands, it was the perfect technique for them. However, that same "perfect" technique may not have been perfect in the other doctor's hands. Additionally, the procedure itself may not have gone perfectly in each case. But still, both outcomes were successful.

Success allows for flexibility. Success can and does happen without perfection. Perfectionism can block success. We all want to keep improving ourselves to become the best we can be. However, none of us will ever become perfect. Perfection is an impossible goal. Perfectionism is destructive. If we always search for or try to achieve perfection, we will never be satisfied or happy with our lives. We will never see ourselves as the successful individual we are. Success can equate to perfection, but perfection does not equate to success.

Becoming the best you that you can be, doing something the best that you can at any given moment, is true success. Many times, "good enough" is exactly "perfect" for the situation. Good enough to get the job done successfully. *Perfectly good enough.* Giving yourself permission to be good enough to be successful is where happiness and joy come from. That, alone, can be so freeing!

I am one who, in the past, would have taken offense at someone changing the words of my writings. What was wrong with them? They perfectly reflect my thoughts and feelings. If you can't see that, then something must be wrong with *you*, not my words. I knew what I was talking about! My perception in the past would have been that if an editor found ways to improve my already "perfect" words, I had failed. My dream of publishing a book would never come to fruition because I was a failure at putting the "right" words down on paper.

I have a very different perspective on that now. It has become fun to have someone pick apart, critique, and help me reword my work. With my beginner's mind, I see how an editor and coach can take the raw words and thoughts I want to share, make suggestions to shift some of my self-perceived perfect words to successful words that will even more effectively communicate my intent. Now, I find that under the skillful guidance of my coach, collaboration is just taking my dreams and bringing them into an even bigger reality than I could have believed possible on my own. I am grateful that I was willing (there's that "willing" word again) to listen to someone else's perspective, allowing me to grow. Without them, this book would not be my second one published, and would likely not exist at all!

In this same way, the skillful guidance of a coach, teacher, colleague, or friend can help improve your communication skills in all aspects of life. Yet another source of happiness.

## Chapter 20

## SELF-CARE IS ESSENTIAL

We often hear that we need to take care of ourselves before we take care of others. I have learned through personal experience that this is true. You can't care for others effectively if you're not taking care of yourself. If your caregiving doesn't include yourself, it's incomplete.

In my work with veterinarians and technicians, I often hear statements like

- "There is no time for me to take care of myself."
- "When I get home, it's so late and I'm so tired I just fall into bed [or] crash with a drink in front of the TV [or] grab junk food on the way home, so I don't have to cook" (Add your own versions here).
- "My workday is so crazy that I never get a break or lunch. If I eat at all, I grab something on the run."

- "My family demands all of my time away from work so there is no 'me' time."
- "It's so hard to get everything done!"
- "It's just too hard to make the effort to change."

At the risk of being repetitive on this very important subject, you can't care for others effectively if you don't take care of yourself.

So why does it feel so impossible to find time to care for yourself? Work-life balance is a buzz phrase that has been grossly overused and has caused considerable damage to many people. It suggests that there should be an even balance between your time, energy, and success at work and at home.

It suggests that if you cannot achieve this, you have failed somehow. In fact, it sets you up for failure because it truly isn't possible to evenly balance your work life and personal life. Reality is a very different thing.

True work-life balance – or better yet, work-life integration – is much more fluid. Work-life integration reflects a much more realistic approach. Integrating all of the various aspects of your life in a manner that works for you is what matters. Again, you have the choice on how you spend every minute of every day (unless you've literally been kidnapped, tied up, and held hostage).

There are times when work will consume you, and appropriately so. Say you are beginning a new practice or joining a practice or team you've never worked with before. Your focus and energy will be on getting yourself established. You may work considerable overtime during this process. Perhaps you are in a practice with multiple veterinarians and one or more are out sick, on vacation, or taking personal time. You will likely put in overtime to cover for the missing staff.

During these times, work will monopolize large portions of your time. Your personal life may take a backseat or feel non-existent. This is the price you pay to build and grow a career that is important and rewarding to you. In these cases, the scale of work-life balance is tilted one way more heavily. It is your choice to do so or not, understanding that the scale will tip the other way at some point, too.

Conversely, there will be times when your personal life will have that balance scale tilted in its direction. Say, for example, you are planning to be married. Your attention may need to be on wedding details, your partner, and your family rather than career details. Or perhaps you have a new child entering the family. Maybe you have a sick family member you need to care for, or your dream vacation is approaching and deserves your undivided attention.

The concept that the scales must be evenly balanced at all times is ridiculous, not to mention impossible. Life ebbs and flows. Sometimes you're up, and sometimes you're down. The key is to accept each stage for what it is. Understand that it is temporary, regardless of the position you are in.

Self-awareness, self-management, and self-care make the ups and downs of life feel more like a natural ebb and flow than a crazy, uncontrolled rollercoaster. Recognizing when things are not going well or are causing stress, and implementing additional self-care techniques is necessary. It is important to schedule time to maximize your physical, mental, emotional, and spiritual health. Remember, self-care doesn't have to be time consuming. Small things, done regularly, can bring substantial relief. Waiting for a good time to do some self-care is also a futile effort. There will never be a "good time" unless you schedule it into your calendar just as you would any appointment. Then, honor that appointment with yourself just as you would an appointment with someone else. You are just as important as that other person is. You are just as important as *any* other person is.

I've been asked if self-care is selfish, as I was taught as a child. I was taught to always think of others first and give to them before taking for myself. In general, that is a good way to approach life, unless it becomes entirely one-way. I've come to believe, through research and my own personal experience, that self-care not only isn't selfish, it's crucial for you to be at your best. For you to be able to give to others, you must have something left inside to give. If you are not willing to receive, you ultimately will have nothing left to give. You cannot pour from an empty cup. To be able to continually give, you must have a ready source for your cup to be refilled.

I've also been asked if you can get too carried away with self-care. I believe there is a difference between deep self-care and excessive self-indulgence. With this in mind, the importance of deep self-care will not be lost.

There may be times when deep self-care can slide into self-indulgence. When this happens, it is often accompanied by a different type of restlessness or dissatisfaction that might relate to feelings of lack of purpose, a feeling of entitlement, or other negative feelings. Recognizing this difference and managing it are important.

There are also times when self-care is a full-time job until healing is done. This is not self-indulgence. It is a necessary thing to bring your body, mind, and/or spirit back into balance. Back into a place where you have something of value to give. Eventually, as healing continues, you will grow back into your life again.

Whether you are doing self-care or have crossed into self-indulgence cannot be judged by others or outside feedback. It must come from you. Recognizing the difference between deep self-care and self-indulgence requires self-awareness. This is the beginning of developing your emotional intelligence (EI/EQ). Emotional intelligence factors heavily in your life success also. I will talk more about emotional intelligence later.

Resilience is the ability to cope in healthy ways despite setbacks, barriers, or limited resources. The ability to bounce back. Resilience often reflects your emotional strength. Resilience can be healthy, or it can be unhealthy. Veterinarians tend to go overboard, priding themselves on how resilient they believe they are. They think they are like the Energizer Bunny who keeps going and going and going. They often believe they should be able to "do it all." After all, they are ultimately responsible for the outcome of what happens under their guidance, aren't they? How often doctors take on the responsibility for things that are completely out of their control!

They forget that, unlike that bunny who can simply have the old batteries removed and new ones quickly inserted to keep going, going, going, veterinarians are human and require a different way to recharge. Their batteries are not replaceable. They indeed must stop and take breaks to recharge! Back to that self-care thing. Take themselves offline for a while to recharge their batteries rather than simply try to replace them with unhealthy substitutions and habits to keep going. A novel concept to many!

Some inadvertently slip into unhealthy coping activities instead of taking time for self-care. A little wine or a shot of whisky to wind down at the end of the day. Plugging in to more coffee or energy drinks during the day to keep them "on top of their game." Going, going, going. This can easily evolve into dangerous coping activities, often without the person realizing they are going down that road.

Then the wall appears. When the mind and body begin to object to the continual demands and abuse. They may think, "I've always been able to do it. Why am I having trouble now? Why can't I seem to do it all anymore? What's wrong with me? My mind used to be able to keep everything straight; now, sometimes I struggle. My body aches in places it shouldn't. My shoulders and back hurt. Why is my stomach always so sensitive now? It seems like I always wake up as tired as when I went to bed."

Daily demands require healthy resilience, compassion, sympathy, and emotional intelligence on the part of the doctor and staff. We are just ordinary people being asked to do extraordinary things. To continue to successfully and joyfully do the things we are asked, we must increase our emotional intelligence and self-care practices. Preferably before we crash.

Chapter 24 provides a selection of self-care and stress reduction techniques for you to use. Try them and see which serves you best. You may find that one works better for you in certain situations than another. Practice will improve each of them.

# Chapter 21

## STRESSORS SPECIFIC TO VETERINARIANS

Why are veterinarians so stressed out?

Recent surveys found that some of the most common and most severe stressors for veterinarians include:

- Finances. School debt is so excessive, that many veterinarians will not be able to pay off their loans during their work-life span. Income for veterinarians is often not commensurate with their training, skills, and knowledge.

- Long hours and increasing workloads. Being away from their family for extended periods of time. Being expected to accomplish even more in a day without any additional support staff to assist.

- Negative work culture or atmosphere. Bosses and/or co-workers who have negative attitudes, complain, fail to show appreciation for work done, cliques, a competitive rather than cooperative atmosphere, and much more can increase stress.

- Increasing expectations from clients. Clients often expect more from their veterinarian than they do from their personal physician. They demand more access, more accountability, and more services – all for less money. Yet, the skills, knowledge, and training required to provide these services are frequently greater than those required by their physician counterparts.

- Bullying by clients in person and on social media. Bullying has become so commonplace and aggressive that veterinarians have committed suicide over it. Veterinarians even get the occasional death threats. I received one from a client years ago. Recently, another veterinarian received a death threat that she wrote about. Her verbal assailant even told her that since he was aware that veterinarians were at a higher risk of suicide, he hoped she would do the right thing and do that to herself.

- Ethical and moral dilemmas that cause distress. Often clients will ask things of a veterinarian that are completely unethical for the doctor to do. Then the client may become upset when the veterinarian appropriately refuses. Other times, the veterinarian may be pushed to do things that go against their moral code. In some cases, they even struggle between maintaining their moral beliefs or their job.

- Emotional distress of loss. Veterinarians face death and loss on a regular basis. They often are emotionally attached to the clients and pets they may have seen since they originally came in for their first well-puppy or kitten check. Frequently, the veterinarian is placed in the position of comforting the pet owner mentally and emotionally while setting aside their own emotions over the loss. Then, they are expected to shake off the situation and move into the next room with the next client joyfully, without having the opportunity to acknowledge their own feelings and grief. (Switching from despair to the elation of a new puppy in the next room causes the mind and body to do major swings in a short period of time.)

- Decision Fatigue. This occurs when the mind has difficulty making even simple decisions because of the number of decisions (often difficult ones) required on a daily basis, both at work and in their personal life.

- Empathic Distress, compassion fatigue, burnout. Empathy is the ability to feel other's emotions and feelings with them. Empathic distress can leave one spiraling downward in suffering along with the client and pet. Withdrawal, poor health, fatigue, and burnout can ultimately occur.

- The natural inclination as a caregiver to give until they drop without the understanding that if they do not include themselves in their caregiving efforts, their caregiving is incomplete.

Veterinarians, staff, and other caregivers in general tend to be altruistic. Altruism may be defined as reactively acting out of concern for another's well-being. When we see someone in desperate circumstances, we often behave altruistically, feeling sympathy or empathy and a desire to help. Acts of altruism activate the reward centers of the brain, which gives people positive feelings about themselves.

People who act in an altruistic way in a given circumstance – for example, by putting themselves at risk in the effort to save another person from a dangerous situation – typically feel the reward internally. But what happens when altruism becomes pathologic? Pathologic altruism is when people show excessive compassion for others to the detriment of themselves, having the tendency to rush in and help when they should hold back. They give day in and day out until there is nothing left of them to give. When this happens, the givers eventually burn out completely.

Many people who choose to spend their lives as caregivers have an increased tendency to slip over the edge from healthy altruism into pathologic altruism.

Understanding the difference between pity, sympathy, empathy, and compassion gives doctors and other caregivers tools to effectively manage their own emotions as well as those of others while they interact with clients, patients, coworkers, and staff.

| Pity | Sympathy | Empathy | Compassion |
|---|---|---|---|
| I acknowledge your suffering. | I care about your suffering. | I feel your suffering with you. | I care for, feel, and want to relieve your suffering. |

## Degree of Emotional Engagement

Pity is the acknowledgement of someone's suffering, but at a distance. Sometimes from a place of superiority.

Sympathy is the ability to care about and understand the suffering of others while remaining grounded and focused in your own feelings. Feeling pity and sorrow for someone else's misfortune. I feel *for* you and care that you are suffering.

Empathy is the ability to actually experience the feelings of another person with them. The ability to put yourself in their place. Empathy goes beyond sympathy in that I feel *with* you rather than *for* you. This connection with others can be a blessing or a painful, unbearable weight, depending on the situation and the empathic individual. Empathy encompasses a broad range of emotional states and types, including cognitive empathy, emotional empathy, and somatic empathy. The empathic person literally feels, to varying degrees, what another person is feeling. As a result, it may become difficult for the empathic person to separate or tell the difference between another's feelings and their own.

## Sympathy or Empathy + A Desire to help = Compassion

Compassion is sympathy or empathy plus a desire to relieve the discomfort someone is experiencing. A person who takes always gives to others and forgets to address their own needs with compassion is setting themselves up for exhaustion and burnout.

## COMPASSION FATIGUE OR EMPATHIC DISTRESS?

While compassion fatigue tends to get more press coverage, empathic distress can be more of an issue than compassion fatigue. Empathic distress is potentially the underlying cause of compassion fatigue, and certainly a contributing factor. The emerging understanding of empathic distress shows that those who suffer from it may be at greater personal risk. Because compassion is the combination of either sympathy or empathy plus the desire to help relieve suffering, those compassionate people coming from an empathic position rather than a sympathetic position seem to be at higher risk for compassion fatigue and burnout.

Empathic people tend to be more sensitive in general than those who are not. Many people in the caregiving services are naturally empathic. In part, it's what draws them into caregiving. Empathy is a wonderful trait to possess. It helps you connect on a deeper level with your clients and patients. However, it often leaves the empathic individual open to experience a deeper level of pain than those who are sympathetic but not empathic.

When these naturally sensitive people choose to enter difficult or frequently challenging situations, such as a veterinary practice, medical school, or as first responders, self-care must be taken seriously. They need to learn tools to effectively protect themselves from empathic distress.

Taking on the emotions of others, as empaths tend to do, on top of one's own natural emotions can be devastating. For me, learning to separate my true feelings from those of others I encountered has been of utmost importance to my survival.

Learning self-protection techniques has also been invaluable. To learn more about self-protection techniques that are actually fun, contact Cynde.

The environment in which caregivers work is important, too. Working in a positive, supportive environment with co-workers who openly appreciate them is ideal. Having clients who appreciate the caregiver's efforts is rewarding.

However, this isn't always possible. Veterinarians and staff may find themselves in working environments that are not supportive. Co-workers may not perform as a cohesive team. Bosses may not encourage or nurture a positive working environment. According to a Gallup Survey, the number-one reason people leave their jobs is because they have a poor relationship with their boss.

Caregivers often lack a positive mirror reflecting back to them their value. In these situations, as mentioned previously, a separate coach or mentor can be extremely useful. This coach or mentor can give unbiased support and guidance, often seeing and pointing out the good that may get overlooked in the daily grind.

There has been a dramatic increase of clients literally bullying veterinarians and their staff in recent years. With the advent of social media, people often feel safe saying things online that they would never say to someone in person. There is a feeling of distance, anonymity, and perceived safety in posting negative remarks online. There is no accountability for their actions. Even if the client retracts their negative comments, the negative comments remain out there for all to see, and the retraction often goes unnoticed. Emotional intelligence offers effective ways to deal with these bullies while maintaining one's sanity.

# Chapter 22

# EMOTIONAL INTELLIGENCE

I have mentioned emotional intelligence a few times. So what is it? Let's touch on that now. Some seasons of life are a rollercoaster, and others are smooth sailing. It's important to develop the emotional intelligence skills of self-awareness, self-management, social awareness, and relationship management so that you can successfully navigate the various seasons life has in store for you.

Increasing your personal emotional intelligence will leave you more effectively prepared to not just survive, but to thrive, even in challenging situations. Individuals with higher emotional intelligence focus better and learn more readily. They interact with others more fluidly and overall perform better than their peers. Once again, this relates back to why some people thrive in their career while others flounder.

Emotional intelligence may be defined in a few different ways.

- Dictionary.com defines it as "the capacity to be aware of, control, and express one's emotions, and to handle interpersonal relationships judiciously and empathetically."
- The Institute for Health and Human Potential (Daniel Goleman) defines it as "the ability to a) recognize, understand, and manage our own emotions; and b) recognize, understand, and influence the emotions of others." In practical terms, this means being aware that emotions can drive behavior and impact people (positively and negatively), and learning how to manage those emotions – both our own and others – especially when we are under pressure.
- Beryl Comar, in her training class, defines it as "the capacity for recognizing our own feelings and those of others, for motivating ourselves [and] for managing emotions well – in ourselves and in our relationships."

And my personal favorite, from *Building Blocks of Emotional Intelligence* by Daniel Goleman: emotional intelligence is "a different way of being smart."

He also states, "Emotional-intelligence based capabilities are twice as important for star performance as IQ and technical skills combined."

Research indicates that the biggest reason that managers fail is poor interpersonal skills; in fact, roughly half of all managers have problems relating to their associates and employees. A lack of emotional intelligence is often the underlying cause.

It is well known that when emotions run the show, communication and rational thinking decrease significantly. This is why advertisers who promote their products by reaching their audiences' emotional level typically sell more. People buy on emotion and then rationalize their purchase later.

Similarly, when people attempt to communicate with emotions

running high, or when the emotions of the other person are high, misunderstandings occur more frequently than when communication occurs during a relaxed or managed state. Learning to identify and manage your personal state at any given time, as well as identifying the state of others, allows you to modify your communication approach so that you will be not only heard, but to have your information resonate in the desired manner.

Emotionally intelligent people show the following traits:

- They are aware of how they feel at any given time.
- They understand how their moods and emotions affect others.
- They can identify what motivates them personally as well as what disheartens them or stalls their progress.
- They communicate well with others. When emotionally intelligent people listen, it is with the intent to understand and to adapt their communication to accommodate the unique needs of others.
- Emotionally intelligent people are less reactive and more responsive, handling stressful situations more calmly and effectively. They respond to changes life throws their way, rather than becoming reactive, frustrated, or overwhelmed by them.
- They have a positive and optimistic mindset. Think back to the previous sections on the benefits of a positive attitude, of starting from a positive mindset rather than a negative one. A positive mental approach energizes you to continue working toward your goals, rather than being discouraged and quitting in the face of setbacks or obstacles.
- They are adaptable. They get creative with their problem-solving tools.

There are four cornerstones, or competencies, to emotional intelligence.[14] They are:

1. self-awareness,

2. self-regulation,
3. social awareness, and
4. relationship management

**Self-Awareness:** Your ability to accurately identify your emotions in the moment and understand your typical response style in unique, challenging situations.

But what are emotions? Emotions are internal, instinctive information and not related to reasoning or knowledge. Emotions are just data. Internal information. What becomes important is how you use that information. How you respond to this internal data can impact your physiology, thoughts, mental health, performance, and relationships. They are based on your internal representation, your own beliefs about what is happening around you. The story we tell ourselves about what we perceive.

When you have good self-awareness, you know what you feel and *why* you are having those feelings. You become aware of how your emotions help or hinder what you are trying to accomplish. As you practice this, you begin to sense how others truly see you, rather than how your internal bias or self-talk may have misled you. With this insight, your self-image becomes more aligned with reality, and you develop an accurate sense of your strengths and limitations. This allows you to develop a realistic self-confidence and gives you clarity on your values and a sense of purpose. It becomes easier to be more decisive, open, and authentic when you set a course of action and communicate it with others.

**Self-Regulation:** Using the awareness of your emotions, that internal data, to positively impact your action and behavior choices.[15]

Emotions can be disruptive when acted on impulsively. It's important to accept that your emotions are real. Emotions are not to be suppressed or ignored. They provide valuable information. It's about remaining clear-headed and calm in the face of your emotions. Again, it's how you choose to interpret, manage, or self-regulate those emotions that will determine your efficacy during stressful or potentially hostile situations.

**Social Awareness:** Recognizing and understanding the emotions and moods of other individuals and entire groups of people.[16]

When working one-to-one or with groups of people, it is important to be able to identify and accept the emotions of others. Every group has a power hierarchy, whether it is formal or informal. Being able to read both individual and group emotions enhances your success as a leader or partner. Understanding the emotions of others allows you greater insight into them. It shows you how the emotions of one or more people in the group impacts the balance of the group. This not only enhances your leadership abilities, but also develops an acceptance by others because you understand them on a different, more personal level. They begin to feel heard.

**Relationship Management:** Putting self-awareness, self-management, and social awareness into action as an inspirational leader. Using these tools effectively provides the ability to inspire and guide others to be their best. It gives staff, partners, children, or groups a meaningful way to communicate and work together more effectively as a team. People become more engaged, which decreases their resistance and makes them want to step up more willingly under your skilled guidance.[17, 18]

It is important to cultivate new habits of emotional intelligence and self-care. I love the word cultivate. So often we think of changing old habits or beliefs and learning new ones as a difficult task. Hard work. Yet, the word cultivate suggests nurturing and caring with the work involved, making it easier and more enjoyable.

Dictionary.com defines cultivation as:

- the action of cultivating land,

- the act of caring for or raising plants, and
- the process of trying to acquire or develop a quality or skill.

Let's discover nurturing and caring ways to cultivate the seeds of change you desire.

Your mind is a fertile garden. Your thoughts, beliefs, values, and knowledge are the seeds that grow there. You are the one who cultivates and nurtures the seeds growing in the garden of your mind. Some seeds have been planted by others, while you choose some of your own to plant. Some seeds turn into beautiful, even brilliant flowers that enhance your life, while others may develop into weeds that pollute your mind. Regardless of how the seeds got there, you have complete control over which seeds you nurture into maturity and which you choose to remove or let wither and die. Do you want to spend your time and energy nurturing positive seeds or negative ones? You need to be aware of what seeds are planted, which ones you are nurturing, and which ones you are not.

You have cultivated your current beliefs, values, qualities, and skills over many years. Considerable practice has gone into this development, whether conscious or unconscious. Often, you are not even aware that you are cultivating these beliefs, values, or skills. You do it unconsciously, based on habit and repetition. When you look more closely and develop your self-awareness, you may discover that you have been inadvertently cultivating unhealthy practices while neglecting healthy ones.

Ask yourself, "Am I planting and cultivating seeds of anger, doubt, antipathy, or worse? Or am I planting and cultivating seeds of compassion, peace, self-care, and kindness?" This is a choice you have. Making kinder, gentler choices for yourself becomes easier when you cultivate and nurture the seeds of kindness and compassion regularly.

In the 2011 movie The *Iron Lady*, Meryl Streep, in her role as Margaret Thatcher, states

- Watch your thoughts, for they become words.
- Watch your words, for they become actions.
- Watch your actions, for they become habits.
- Watch your habits, for they become your character.
- And watch your character, for it becomes your destiny.
- What we think, we become.[19]

There are many versions of this quote in use today, attributed to many authors. The important point of this passage is that everything starts with your thoughts. What you spend time thinking about ultimately becomes your destiny. Repetition of anything – thought, action or habit – makes it a fixture in your life. This can be good or bad, depending on what you choose to think, repeat, and nurture.

### Patience and practice are your allies.

It has taken me time, patience, failure, humility, tenacity, and a willingness to become the beginner each day to make the changes I wanted in my life. I still am, and will always be, a work in progress. I continue to use the concepts and tools I've introduced here to maintain the progress I've made and to ensure that my choices stay in line with my values and personal needs.

If you have done the suggested exercises from this book as you've been reading, you have taken the time to identify those beliefs and values that are congruent with who you are. If you haven't completed the exercises yet, consider going back and working through some of them now. The information, exercises, and suggestions given here are intended as a starting point to encourage positive change. Regardless of whether you wish to make just a few changes in your life or desire a significant make-over, take that first step and begin. Remember that reaching out for help is not a sign of weakness; it's a sign of strength, commitment, and devotion to this precious life you have been given.

Once you have begun this rewarding process of change, it is

important to cultivate (care for, nurture, and raise) these new beliefs, values, and skills into a thriving new you. Who will you cultivate yourself to be? It's no different than cultivating a plant. For a plant to be successful, it needs care and nurturing. For you to be successful, you require care and nurturing. Be very selective and specific with your thoughts as you cultivate the future you. The you that you have been longing to become.

## WHEN YOU KNOW WHAT YOU DON'T WANT, YOU KNOW WHAT YOU DO WANT

But what if you're still not sure exactly what you want in life? I am amazed when I ask someone what they want in life, and they typically respond with what they don't want. I see this in clients daily. They are so fixated on what they don't like in their lives that what they want seems elusive or impossible to imagine. Their entire focus is on what they come to me to change or eliminate, without a clear picture of where they want to go.

If you don't know where you are going, you'll never get there. It's easier to identify what you don't like or want because it bothers you.

In previous iterations of myself, that was the only way I could think or respond. The only thing I understood was what I didn't like in my life. The negative, painful parts I wanted to be rid of. It's still something I struggle with occasionally. But as I've practiced focusing on what I want, now and in the future, I am achieving goals that I would have previously considered impossible.

There seems to be an inherent safety in stating what we don't want rather than expressing what we do want. Why doesn't it feel "safe" to ask for what we want in life? Are we afraid of failing to achieve our desires and thus feeling "less than?" Is it because we don't want to be perceived as selfish or greedy? Are we afraid if we ask for what we want, it will forever remain just out of our reach? Will it be taken away? These are very prevalent ways of thinking.

Answering the question "What do you want in your life?" may be one of the most difficult yet rewarding tasks you ever achieve. When you know what you don't want, though, you can begin to use that same information to discover what you do want. This is a universal truth. What is the opposite of what you currently have or want to avoid? Turn what you know you don't want around 180 degrees, and it will point you in the direction of what you do want. Then, you have something to work with. Something to build on. A place to start outlining and then clearly stating what you do want. Once you have clearly stated what you do want, you can then cultivate that and begin to make the changes necessary to move you in the direction of the life you desire.

And, once again, you automatically begin retraining the Reticular Activating System to search for and find ways to achieve what you do want instead of what you don't want. Remember that just as you were specific about what you don't want in your life, you must be very specific in describing what you do want so the RAS can do its job to serve you.

**At this point, you may be thinking, "So... What do I do now? I know something must give, but I don't know how to start, and I'm afraid of change. I'm afraid of messing up even more. How do I get the tools I need to make the changes I want?"**

## Chapter 23

## YOUR TOOLBOX FOR CHANGE

**Let's start building a resource toolbox for you now.**

The primary question is, are you *willing* to make the necessary changes to create the life you desire? Without willingness, coupled with intentional action, your efforts will be futile. You will just spin your wheels. Let's develop some traction and get those changes happening now!

Leaving the profession is, of course, one option to make changes and possibly heal yourself. For some people, this may well be the best choice. If this is your choice, it is still important to develop your emotional intelligence skills so that you are better prepared to deal with the challenges that life, in general, will throw at you. Emotional intelligence development is the foundation for successful life change. You also must be specific in stating what you do want as we've discussed above, or you will just bounce from one unhappy situation to the next, regardless of the field you are in. Remember that the RAS is always listening to you, so feed it the specifics of what you want.

But what if you don't want to leave your profession? How can you make the changes needed to heal yourself and stay with your passion career? What are some ways you can continue forward in a more satisfying way? Find personal, emotional, and professional satisfaction?

Veterinarians are intelligent, analytical, and often complicated people. We've been trained to use critical thinking and analyze everything. When people use this ingrained training in their approach to change, it can feel like a daunting task. Where to start? How to start? What if it's just too hard? There is so much to consider!

This is why The BRAIN System™ is so effective. It breaks a potentially complicated process down into simple steps. Simple steps for the complicated people we are. Remember that these steps really are simple, even if they are not always easy. Choose to begin, and commit to being persistent and patient. Don't try to implement everything at once; it will frankly make things difficult and complicated again.

## IMPLEMENTING The BRAIN System™

The BRAIN System™ is a step-by-step framework to guide you in the process of changing your life into one that you desire and enjoy. It is designed in this specific order to enhance the change process. The steps are as follows:

**B**elieve that you can make positive changes in your life using your own mind. Indulge me a bit here. You don't have to fully believe this yet. Initially, all you need is a willingness to believe that believing in your ability to make the changes you desire is possible. That is enough to get you started. You may have been trying to change your life for years without the results you wanted. You simply didn't have the tools you needed. You have access to those tools now. Keep that willingness alive and believe that by implementing these simple steps, it will happen for you.

$R$elease anything that no longer serves you. The best place to start is with self-awareness, the first competency in emotional intelligence. Pay attention to the quality of your thoughts. As you become aware of how you talk to yourself, you will develop an understanding of how you reached the place you are in today. If your thoughts are mostly positive, more power to you! Keep it up, working on small tweaks to continually improve them! If, however, you notice that your thoughts tend to be more on the negative or critical side, this self-awareness will open opportunities for you to look at different, more positive ways to approach things. Make it a game to notice how you talk to yourself, and see how many of your old, unhelpful practices you can release. Give yourself points for every item you release that no longer serves you. Watch those points build up!

$A$djust. Make small, powerful adjustments to what you are already doing to get big results. Keep it simple here. Pick one small thing that triggers a negative reaction in you. Get creative, use that powerful imagination of yours, and come up with a way to adjust one thing at a time so that it no longer triggers you into negativity. It doesn't have to suddenly turn from a negative trigger into something that gives you joy, just a small change that takes the sting out of the situation. Remember that you are making small adjustments regularly to ultimately decrease the overall negativity, thus improving your quality of life.

$I$nstall new perceptions, beliefs and habits. Start looking at both positive and negative experiences with curiosity rather than judgment. The more you practice being curious, the easier it becomes. Remember to be curious and comfortable rather than judgmental and uncomfortable. Eventually, you will find yourself skipping over the negative perceptions in favor of curiosity and learning. Use this not only for situations around you, but also for your own self-talk. Ask yourself, with curiosity, why you chose that particular wording or tone to talk to yourself. Talking to yourself with positive, reinforcing words and attitudes is crucial. Find kinder, gentler ways to speak to yourself.

**N**europlasticity. Enjoy the benefits as you sustainably reprogram or rewire your brain to see and feel happiness and joy. This is another example of perspective. When you practice looking specifically for the positive things around you, you automatically notice more of them. You are literally rewiring your brain to perceive more of the good and less of the negative. That's not to say that there isn't always negative and positive around you. While it may be important to acknowledge the negative at times, it's a matter of what you choose to *focus* on and bring more of into your life. When you choose to focus on even the smallest good things around you, it shifts your perspective. The shift may be slow, or it may happen quickly. That is entirely up to you. However, right here, right now, you can choose to start.

## Summary: Small, Steady Changes = Big Results

Sustainable change doesn't happen if you try to do it all at once or in big chunks. Small, incremental changes, implemented consistently, will lead to your success. You don't have to throw your whole life out to make major, valuable changes. The success of these small, incremental changes will lead to the big changes you desire. The changes must feel and be doable. Be compassionate with yourself as you go through this process. Remember, it's progress, not perfection.

The BRAIN System™ guides you through the simple process of tapping onto the unlimited power of your own mind to make lasting, positive change. It gives you tools that you can use throughout your life. Again, self-directed neuroplasticity. In other words, you learn how to use simple tools to literally rewire your brain. For more information on how to implement The Brain System™ go to www.brightpaths.com and schedule your complimentary discovery session.

The tools provided in this book, when applied consistently, can help you significantly reduce negative stress and overcome fears or limiting beliefs that impact your life.

What if you could feel good in your own skin again? And maybe fall in love with veterinary medicine – or life – again?

Using Old Skills in New Ways

It bears repeating that your imagination is the most powerful life tool you have in your toolbox. Use it and use it wisely. Worry is a misuse of your imagination, the result of consistent focus on a *potential* negative outcome. The stronger your innate ability to focus, the deeper your worry. If you are a "worry wort" like me, you have a very strong ability to focus. Unfortunately, this strong ability to focus has been directed toward the negative things your imagination has created for you, rather than the positive. It's time to shift that strong focusing ability, now.

You have already proven that you can use your imagination extremely effectively to create critical, disempowering, and judgmental thoughts and scenarios. Those stories you tell yourself. Begin now to use this well-developed, finely-tuned skill you are already proficient at to imagine new, empowering, positive scenarios that you desire. Now *that* is an effective use of the imagination.

## Remember: Possibility is unlimited!

The only limit to possibility is your imagination. Since there is no limit to your imagination, the only limits are the ones your own imagination places there. How's that for a paradox? The bottom line is to allow your imagination to dream big without limits. You now know that if you can imagine a negative outcome, you can also imagine a positive one. Where will you focus your amazing imagination?

I have enjoyed wonderful changes in my life since I chose to accept life on life's terms. Once I became willing and open to new perspectives, I have continued to develop my own emotional intelligence. I have a long way to go, but the journey has become so much more enjoyable. When did my life change? When I made a *choice* that night while watching the ceiling fan turn. When I accepted that I couldn't, wouldn't go on the way things were. **When I became willing and open to change**.

When will you choose to change? When will you become willing and open? I certainly hope it is soon. Please don't wait until you get to the desperate point I reached. When you do make the choice, what's going on inside you and what's going on around you will also change. Have the courage to open yourself up and be willing to change. I'm speaking from experience. It's worth it!

## FIND A COACH OR MENTOR

Working with a coach or mentor is one of the most effective and fastest ways to create desired change in your life. A coaching relationship provides an environment of emotional safety in which to grow and is a safe place to explore and make mistakes. To test out new ideas. It becomes easier to identify what might be holding you back, thereby allowing you to move forward with positive change.

If you want significant change in your life, give yourself the gift of a coach to help you open the doors to a new and satisfying future. For more details on working with Cynde to change your life, go to www.brightpaths.com and schedule a free discovery session.

# Chapter 24

# Stress Reduction Practices

## Breathing Techniques

There is a reason why breathing techniques for stress reduction are so prevalent in many cultures, and why most self-help/self-care programs include them. They are simple, you can do them anywhere and anytime, and they work. Healthy breathing exercises can help:

- increase blood flow to the cells, improving brain function;
- decrease stress levels, calming the nervous system;
- relax tense muscles;
- act as a natural painkiller (I personally use a specific directed breathing program to manage pain, either acute or chronic);
- increase energy levels, creating a refreshing effect;
- improve posture;

- reduce inflammation;
- stimulate lymphatic system;
- detoxify the body; and
- improve digestion, triggering the rest and digest phase.

The simplest breathing technique is to breathe in deeply for four counts, hold the breath for six counts, then exhale deeply for eight counts. As few as three consecutive deep breaths like this has been shown to significantly decrease stress levels, increase oxygen to all cells, and decrease discomfort.

Remember to expand your belly as you inhale, allowing your diaphragm to move down freely. Notice how the muscles between the ribs expand, moving your ribcage out. Give those lungs room to fill completely!

The exhale is just as important – and possibly more important – than the inhale. As you exhale, force out the last bits of air so there is plenty of room for fresh air to fill your lungs. This also forces any toxins to be expelled from the lungs.

You can do this technique anywhere. Structured breathing practices such as this, when practiced regularly, have shown long term, positive health effects.

Counting your breaths while breathing naturally for ten counts is another technique that increases your ability to focus.

**Bilateral Brain Stimulation (adapted from *The Anti-anxiety Toolkit – Rapid Techniques to Rewire the Brain* by Melissa Tiers)**

This is another simple tool you can use any time you feel stress building – one that you can use to change your state and significantly reduce or eliminate anxiety. The simplicity and effectiveness of this technique may surprise you.

Pick up a pen, your keys, or something else that you can easily pass back and forth between your hands. Hold it in your right hand. Think of something that causes you stress or anxiety – something that really upsets you. When you can feel that stress building, notice where you feel it in your body. Rate that feeling on a scale of zero to ten, with zero being not stressful at all and ten being extremely stressful. For practice, please choose something that rates a six or above on the scale.

Now pass the item you are holding from your right hand to the left, making sure the passing hand crosses the mid-line of your body. In this first step, your right hand will cross the center line of your body before placing the item into the left hand.

Swing the receiving left hand out to the side. Bring the left hand back in and cross the centerline, passing the item back to the right hand and swing the right hand out to the side. Do this back and forth, from one hand to the other, for a minute or so. Stop and take a deep breath. As you exhale, think about how you feel. You will likely note that the sensation of stress or anxiety has decreased. Repeat this process until the anxious feelings have significantly reduced or disappeared.

The reason this works is that anxiety sits in one portion of the brain and gathers significant blood flow and electrical signals to focus on it. When passing an object back and forth in the way you just did, you activate both hemispheres of the brain, spreading blood flow and electrical impulses more evenly throughout the whole brain. Without the focused blood supply and electrical signals, stress automatically dissipates, and the mind becomes relaxed and comfortable.

One executive benefitted so much from this technique that she taught it to her staff. She chuckled as she saw more and more of her employees walking around the office passing pens back and forth between their hands. Then, she began to notice how much more smoothly staff meetings ran.

A variation on this technique works great if you are sitting at a table or desk and need to do a quick stress reduction without being noticed.

Take your right hand and tap your left thigh. Use your left hand to tap your right thigh. Alternate the tapping, right, left, right, left. This can be done subtly and is surprisingly effective in defusing stress and anger.

Each of these techniques works well in business meetings and personal relationships, especially when implemented at the first sign of tension rising.

## Wet Dog Shake™

This is a fun exercise that I created specifically with veterinarians and their staff in mind. Think about a dog who has just gotten out of a scuffle with another dog, and how they give themselves a good, all-over shake. They may even tremble for a bit and shake themselves off to change their state. Animals do this instinctively to "shake off" the effects of previous encounters, especially negative ones.

Start by standing up and moving your shoulders around to loosen them. Now shake yourself off thoroughly. Just like that dog, start with your head and shake your body all the way to your tail. Remember those legs, arms, feet, and hands. Shake off any negative or stagnant energy. Imagine you can see all negativity flying off of you like water droplets. Come on! Get silly with it! Shake it! Now Laugh.

How did that feel? You feel different, don't you? Your energy shifted. There's a reason why the expression "shake it off" came about, as it refers to getting rid of something unpleasant or undesirable and moving on. Shake it off is still used regularly because it is so effective.

Use this activity, giving your body a good shake like a wet dog, as you come out of one exam room or meeting and before you go into the next. Do you think that shaking off the stress of the previous meeting, client, or pet might help you shift gears so that you can be more present with the next one?

Imagine being able to focus more effectively on each situation without stress building and adding to that from any previous encounter!

What about the secondary benefit of changing the state in your staff who see you shaking yourself off like a wet dog? Think they might laugh at you? Even if they just shake their head and think, "Doc's really lost it this time," you are injecting a little humor into the day. Even brief moments of comic relief in an otherwise stressful day can bring about huge positive changes in the entire work environment.

## Begin immediately changing and reprogramming your filters

This requires that you do a little planning ahead. Take a moment and think about a *minimum* of three positive things you can say about yourself. Big or small things, it doesn't matter at this point. Just three good things you know to be true. Write them down in the form "I am…" That's it for the planning ahead work!

Now, as you go about your normal day, pay attention to how you talk to yourself. Become aware of the type of things you say to yourself. Notice if you tend to talk in a positive, sarcastic, or negative way. The next time you catch yourself saying something sarcastic or negative to yourself, no matter how big or insignificantly small it may seem, immediately repeat the three good things you wrote down. Whenever possible, say them out loud.

Practice this simple process regularly, and you will not only notice negative self-talk more readily, you will find it less comfortable. Ask yourself how you might have said that in a kinder way. As you practice, you will begin to catch yourself *before* you say the negative thing. It will become natural for you to automatically choose positive wording. With time, this will spill over into your daily interactions with others, and you will notice people responding to you more positively.

Again, a simple, yet profound change process.

To learn more about the programs Cynde offers and additional books by her, go to www.brightpaths.com

To receive periodic tips and tricks to enhance your life and career satisfaction, and receive a free digital copy of the <u>Veterinarian's Cheat Sheet for Leaving Work at Work and Eliminating the Guilt,</u> go to: https://brightpaths.lpages.co/cheat-sheet

# References:

1.  Hammond, D.C. (2010). Hypnosis in the treatment of anxiety- and stress-related disorders. Expert Review of Neurotherapeutics, 10(2), 263-273. Doi:10.1586/ern.09.140

2.  Richardson, J., Smith, J.E., et al. (2006). Hypnosis for Procedure-related Pain and Distress in Pediatric Cancer Patients: A systematic Review of Effectiveness and Methodology Related to Hypnosis Interventions. Journal of Pain and Symptom Management, 31(1), 70-84. Doi:10.1016/j.jpainsymman.06.010

3.  Jensen, M.P. (2009). Hypnosis for chronic pain management: A new hope. Pain, 146(3), 235-237. Doi:10.1016/j.pain.2009.06.027

4.  Riehl, M.E., & Keefer, L. (2015). Hypnotherapy for Esophageal Disorders. American Journal of Clinical Hypnosis, 58(1), 22-33. Doi:10.1080/00029157.2015.102\

5.  Ruzyla-Smith, P., Barabasz, A., et al. (1995) Effects of Hypnosis on the Immune Response: B-Cells, T-Cells, Helper and Suppressor Cells. American Journal of Clinical Hypnosis, 38(2), 71-79. Doi:10.1080/00029157.1995.10403185

6.  Dyer, W.W., Change Your Thoughts-Change Your Life: Living the Wisdom of the Tao, (2007) Hay House

7.  Govender, Serusha, Is the Nocebo Effect Hurting Your Health?, WebMD Archives

8. Nayana Ambardekar, Webmd.com – Health & Balance > Stress Management, How to Manage Stress, Reviewed on June 13, 2020

9. Protect Your Brain from Stress, Harvard Health Publishing, Harvard Medical School, health.harvard.edu, *Harvard Women's Health Watch*

10. doctoroz.com, Home > Article > Dr. Oz's Ultimate Stress Checklist.

11. Stress-induced cognitive dysfunction: hormone-neurotransmitter interactions in the prefrontal cortex by Rebecca M. Shansky and Jennifer Lipps, Laboratory of Neuroanatomy and Behavior, Department of Psychology, Northeastern University, Boston, MA, Front. Hum. Neurosci., 05 April 2013    https://doi.org/10.3389/fnhum.2013.00123

12. Textbook of Clinical Neurology (Third Edition), 2007, The Reticular Activating System

13. Stress, Cleveland Clinic Articles, https://my.clevelandclinic.org/health/articles/11874-stress

14. *Building Blocks of Emotional Intelligence: Emotional Self Awareness: A Primer,* by Daniel Goleman, Richard Boyatzis, Richard J. Davidson, Vanessa Druskat, George Kohlrieser.

15. *Building Blocks of Emotional Intelligence: Emotional Self Control: A Primer,* by Daniel Goleman, Richard Boyatzis, Richard J. Davidson, Vanessa Druskat, George Kohlrieser.

16. *Building Blocks of Emotional Intelligence: Organizational Awareness: A Primer,* by Daniel Goleman, Richard Boyatzis, Richard J. Davidson, Vanessa Druskat, George Kohlrieser.

17. *Building Blocks of Emotional Intelligence: Inspirational Leadership: A Primer,* by Daniel Goleman, Richard Boyatzis, Richard J. Davidson, Vanessa Druskat, George Kohlrieser.

18. *Building Blocks of Emotional Intelligence: Influence: A Primer,* by Daniel Goleman, Richard Boyatzis, Richard J. Davidson, Vanessa Druskat, George Kohlrieser.

19. 2011, Movie: The Iron Lady, Director: Phyllida Lloyd, Screenplay Writer: Abi Morgan, Playing Margaret Thatcher: Meryl Streep, Production Comanies: Pathé, Film4, UK Film Council. (Quoted script lines from Meryl Streep as Margaret Thatcher begin at approximately 52 minutes

# About the Author

## Hi, I'm Cynde,

I am on a mission to transform the lives of veterinarians and other professionals. To nurture positive change. As a retired veterinarian, it breaks my heart to see the crisis of excessive stress, depression and suicide that plagues veterinarians and their staff.

A serious car accident resulted in a chronic pain syndrome where I lost much of the use of my right arm and hand. This effectively ended my career as a practicing veterinarian. After years of depression, pain, and wanting to end it all, I discovered the power of the mind-body connection.

I founded Bright Paths, a hypnotherapy, stress reduction and integrative success coaching practice to support others dealing with challenging life situations. Combining the skills and experience from my veterinary years with my years as a board-certified hypnotist and integrative success coach, I have developed simple, powerful and sustainable lifetime tools that can be used to reduce stress and create positive change, helping professionals reignite their passion for life.

**Are you ready to move your life <u>From Frazzled to Dazzled</u>?**
**Reach out to me, I am a resource for you.**

## CYNDE GARDNER, DVM, BCH
### INTEGRATIVE SUCCESS COACH

www.brightpaths.com

(800) 278-0659

Printed in Great Britain
by Amazon

84306473R00088